MY
STORY

MY LIFE AND TIMES

MY STORY

MY LIFE AND TIMES

BY ALLEN A. LENIUS

As told to
Sue, Steve, Betsy, Chris, Angie, and Becky

Christmas 2014

NELSON BORHEK PRESS • MINNEAPOLIS, MINNESOTA

ISBN: 978-1503395404

Nelson Borhek Press
Minneapolis, Minnesota

Printed in the United States of America

CONTENTS

PART II
Meditations

DEDICATION

This book is lovingly dedicated to the memory of:

ALBERT RUDOLPH LENIUS, my father,
    Who taught me how to drive,
    Who took me deer hunting,
    Who built a cottage called "Sleepy Hollow" for me
      to enjoy while I was growing up.

EVA NELSON LENIUS, my mother,
    Who made all my clothes while I was growing up,
    Who cut my hair and pulled my teeth,
    Who walked me to kindergarten each day
      and back again,
    Who gave me food, clothes and support
      my whole life long.

NORMAN ALFRED LENIUS, my brother,
    Who taught me electricity, chemistry, woodworking,
      handling a rope, first aid, leatherworking,
      handicrafts, fixing things, how to fly a kite, and
      so much more.

And — in honor of my six children, for all the
happiness they have given me:

    SUSAN MARIE (Sue) LENIUS (Dreydoppel)
    STEPHEN ALBERT LENIUS
    ELIZABETH ANN (Betsy) LENIUS (Wingren)
    CHRISTOPHER ALLEN LENIUS
    ANGELA JOY (Angie) LENIUS (Neal)
    REBECCA KAY (Becky) LENIUS (McKeever)

Each of you is so gifted, and have used your gifts well.
I could not be more proud of what you have become.
And to each of you, my gratitude and love.

MY STORY

MY LIFE AND TIMES

PREFACE

It all began in a strawberry patch. Just one hundred years ago, my father was picking strawberries in my mother's father's strawberry patch. And as human nature took its course, on June 20, 1917, the minister of the Sturgeon Bay Moravian Church came out to Little Harbor to perform the wedding of Albert Lenius and Eva Nelson, my father and mother. Had that not occurred, I would not be here to tell the story. Incidentally, another wedding was held in Nasewaupee on May 8, 1919, when Hartha Lenius was wed to Olaf Nelson. That, too, began in the same strawberry patch.

Historians today are urging older folk to record the story of their lives, either by using new technology or on paper, so this information can be held for posterity. To this end, while I'm still able to use my red IBM Selectric II with self-correcting tape, I give you—"My Story."

PART I

CHAPTER 1

HOW IT ALL BEGAN

In the late 1880s, four Lenius brothers came to Door County. All four of them bought farms close to one another in the Nasewaupee area just south of Sturgeon Bay, near the waters of Green Bay. Each of them, Herman, Rudolph, Henry and Frank, began farming and raising families.

Herman was married to Augusta Dombrowsky. They had a family of four boys and five girls. The first one, born in 1890, was my father, Albert. The other children and their spouses were: Lydia (Goodwin Westbay), Oscar (Ethel Viste), Hartha (Olaf Nelson), Martha (Elmer Leege), Frieda (Louis Peters), Erwin, never married, Herbert (Grace), and Ida (Joe Goodwin).

Herman's home was near Sand Bay, on the waters of Green Bay (just past the Yogi Bear trailer park). The home is still there. (I have been on the property but never found the owners of it at home when I was there.) Their children went to school a mile away (the school is now a home, painted yellow), and their church was near the school. It was an Evangelical church, which is now a wedding chapel. It is located on what now is Lenius Road.

My father said that he quit school after the second grade. His teacher only spoke English and he only understood German, so he quit. This may not be literally true, but it shows that school did not make a big impression on him. As the oldest boy on a farm, there was plenty for him to do at home. He told me that frequently Indians would come to their house to trade; the Indians wanted eggs and other food they could not produce themselves, and they offered animal skins or other things that they had.

At one point, my father bought an Edison phonograph with circular rolls. He took it to parties where the people were entertained by the music. This is the phonograph that was in the cottage for many years. My dad also had a motorcycle when he was young, but he got rid of it when he was married.

My mother was born in Little Harbor. Little Harbor is located seven miles north of Sturgeon Bay on the Bay Shore Road. It is the first harbor north of the old stone quarry. In 1880, it had no inhabitants.

Andrew Nelson was born in Sweden in 1852. He was a commercial fisherman in Sweden, but looking for new adventures, he migrated to America some time around 1885 at the age of 33. Since he wanted to continue fishing, he was looking for a place where he could be on the water, and where land was still available. The area of the Great Lakes drew his eye, and Door County in Wisconsin in particular. When he found Little Harbor and found that land was available, he homesteaded a large tract consisting of a long strip of land along what is now Bay Shore Drive and all of the land that goes out to the point. He built a home for himself, a house which still exists and was owned and occupied for many years by Dolores Flok. He also dug a canal inland so that he could bring his boats out of the rough waters to unload fish and to store his boats along an inland dock.

Andrew had left behind in Sweden a younger brother, Hans, who was born in 1864, twelve years younger than himself. So in 1888, when Hans was now 21, Andrew invited his younger brother to come to America and join him in his fishing venture. Hans was here just a short time when he sent money to Sweden to his girl friend, Anna Olson, so she could come over to America and join them. Shortly after she arrived, Hans and Anna were married by the Moravian minister, Rev. Sam Groenfeldt, in Sturgeon Bay.

Hans and Anna built a home for themselves near the water's edge right at the center of Little Harbor, the home now owned and occupied by Michael Gabert. And they began having their family: first a son, Olaf; and then two daughters: Alma, who became Mrs. Frank Nelson; and Eva, my mother, who became Mrs. Albert Lenius. Then there was a son, Alfred, who died in infancy, who was followed by two more daughters: Anna Nelson, who never married; and Lilly, who became Mrs. William Jirtle.

As the family grew, so did the need for a larger house, so Hans built a new home up from the water and across the road, the home now owned and occupied by Harvey Jorns, Jr. As the family grew, there came time for school. The public school, Town of Sevastopol District No. 8, was located up on the top of the bluff and a couple of miles south. The children had to walk about three miles to school each day. But since the teacher in their little one-room school, whose name was James Langemak, usually boarded with the Nelsons, they had the pleasure of walking to school with their teacher each morning.

The school building is still standing, located on a road presently called Bluff Court, but it is in very decrepit condition. The last time I was there a few years ago, the building had been used for the storage of new tin cans to be used for the packing of 50 pounds of frozen cherries.

While the children were still young, Olaf contacted polio. Since their mother was too busy with farm and house work, my mother Eva took a year off from school to take care of Olaf. Eva graduated from the eighth grade in 1910 at the age of 16, and she was one of the top six graduates in the entire county for that year.

Meanwhile the brothers continued their fishing business. In the summer they fished from boats, and in the winter they fished from the ice. One way they fished through the ice was with the use of gill nets. These were long nets, perhaps 80 feet long and 10 feet wide. They had wooden floats attached to the top edge and iron weights attached to the bottom edge. They would chop a series of holes in the ice in a straight line, perhaps 25 feet apart. Then they would have a long stick 30 or more feet long with a rope attached to one end. They would feed the stick under the ice from one hole to the next, pulling the rope along with it. When they got to the end, they would pull the rope across the entire span, pulling the net with it. This was called setting the net. Fish, not seeing the net, would swim into it, getting caught by their gills in the webbing of the net, and they were stuck. The next day, the fishermen would come out and lift the net, removing the fish as they pulled the net from the hole in the ice.

Sometimes the fish could be sold in Sturgeon Bay, but often they had to go farther to sell their catch. My mother,

Eva, told me of the time she went with her father, Hans, in a horse-drawn sled across the ice to Marinette to sell fish. The entire body of water of Green Bay was frozen over, and in those days there was no car-ferry to break through the ice each day. It was there in Marinette that she saw her first motion picture. It probably was one of the new "nickelodeon" theaters which spread across the country beginning in 1905. The film was black and white, and silent. But each theater had either an organ or a piano to provide the accompaniment. And the price of admission? One nickel.

In its earliest days, Sturgeon Bay had a sewing and dressmaking school, offering young ladies the opportunity to learn to become seamstresses. It was owned and operated by my mother. While still a girl, Eva taught herself to sew, and she made most of her own clothes as well as clothes for members of her family. After finishing eighth grade, she began sewing for other families. She lived for a time with the Gietner family (now Birmingham's Bar and Supper Club), making clothes for members of that family. A little later, she took a boat up to Ephraim and lived at the Anderson Hotel. There she waited on tables for the hotel guests at meal times and during the rest of the day she sewed clothes for members of the owners' families, the Andersons and the Valentines. She used to tell me how Everett Valentine would come in and entertain her by his singing as she was sewing clothes for the family.

When the season was over and she returned to Sturgeon Bay, she found a sewing school owned by Mary Weise, a lady from Chicago. After Eva had been in school there a short time, Mary Weise decided to return to

Chicago, so she sold the shop and school to my mother. The school was located on the second floor of the old Washburn Department Store, later Prange-Washburn's, then Prange's, and now Younkers. In those days, there were not a lot of ready-made clothes available, and they were limited in size and styles, so much of the material had to be altered. My mother's shop did all the altering for Washburn's store, and to help her do this, she took in young ladies to train to become seamstresses. She took in as many as four at a time, and these girls boarded with her, and ate meals and slept up there in her quarters. Not only did they learn to alter clothing, but they also learned to make clothes from scratch, to go from a bolt of fabric to a finished article of clothing. Shirts, trousers, dresses, underclothing—all could be made from start to finish, including many very exclusive wedding dresses.

My mother ran the school and shop for a few years, from about 1913 to 1917. Then, before her marriage to Albert Lenius from Nasewaupee in 1917, she sold the shop. However, she never forgot her sewing skills, and throughout her life, she made most of the clothes she wore. When my brother Norman and I were small, she made every stitch of clothing that we wore, inner wear as well as outerwear. And she could sew anything. If we could draw a picture of it, she could sew it. She made us wall tents, with a two-foot wall going straight up on both sides before arching off towards the center, and she made these out of old 100-pound flour sacks, likely that she had bought at Washburn's. When we were Boy Scouts, she made us knapsacks to go camping with, long before anyone other than Boy Scouts were wearing backpacks.

She made a sail for a boat for Warren Sautebin, covers for camping equipment, boxes and bags for this and that. She made me a traveling shaving and toiletries kit that I still use when traveling. We Moravian ministers have a special white robe that we wear for communion, baptisms, confirmations and weddings. They are very complicated to make, but when Vernon Graf's surplice began to show signs of wear, he asked her to make him a new one. So while she was at it, she made me a new one, too, which I still use.

When my father died in 1951, in order to support herself, she again opened up her seamstress shop in our home. Some of the most well-to-do ladies in the area came to our home to have clothes altered, or to have things like wedding dresses made from scratch. Eva passed away in 1997, at the age of 103.

Whenever I come to Sturgeon Bay and walk down 3rd Avenue, which is still Cedar Street to me, I can't help but see the name Washburn's on the front of the store, and up there on the second floor, her sewing shop and school, with all the young ladies my mother taught to become seamstresses.

Andrew never married. But Hans had a growing family to support, so he did other things in addition to fishing. He worked at the stone quarry just down the road, for which he was paid fifty cents a day. He also worked for Reynolds Cherry Orchards. And he did some of his own farming. Among other things, he raised strawberries. And therein lies one of the most important portions in the history of Little Harbor.

One of my mother's sisters, Alma, went to "normal" school and became a teacher. As it happened, she was assigned to teach at a little one-room school, District No. 4 in the town of Nasewaupee. Most of her students had the last name of Lenius because four Lenius brothers had settled there and were farming in that area. One day Alma mentioned to her students that her father, Hans, out in Little Harbor, was in need of people to pick strawberries. This word got to the home of Herman and Augusta Lenius, and their children decided to go to Little Harbor and earn some extra money by picking strawberries. Among those who decided to go was Albert Lenius, the oldest child of Herman and Augusta, born in 1890. There in the strawberry patch the Lenius family met the Nelson family, and Albert Lenius first met Eva Nelson, who had been born in 1894. For a year or two, things took their course until, in the summer of 1917, a wedding was held at Little Harbor uniting Albert Lenius with Eva Nelson, my father and mother. Just a year and a half later, another wedding was held, this time in Nasewaupee, uniting Olaf Nelson, Eva's brother, with Hartha Lenius, Albert's sister. What strange and wonderful things can happen in a strawberry patch.

Soon after they were married, my parents bought a home at 414 Leonhardt Street in Sturgeon Bay. Both of them lived in that house the rest of their lives. The address was later changed to 422 North 5th Place, but it is the same home where our family lived for many years.

2

THE COTTAGE

In 1931, when I was four years old, we built the cottage. By this time, Frank and Alma Nelson had purchased my grandfather Han's farm. My mother's sister, Alma, had borrowed $50 from my mother. Alma asked if instead of repaying the $50, my mother would like a piece of land on the farm, a 50-foot strip of waterfront 250 feet deep. My parents agreed, and the lot was deeded to us. Now Frank had an old grainery building that was unused. So he offered to give it to us if we wanted to move it down to our lot. One Sunday afternoon we gathered some of the relatives to help us move the grainery. But after we had moved it about 20 feet, the whole building collapsed. Now what to do? They decided to take the building apart, board by board, and use the boards to build a cottage. So they moved the boards down to our lot. They took out all the nails, and it became my job to straighten all the nails with a hammer on a piece of railroad track so the nails could be reused. My Uncle Oscar, my dad's brother, was a carpenter, so he volunteered to head up the job. When they thought it over, they decided to buy new boards for the cottage, and use the old boards for the outhouse and trailer shed. The next Sunday afternoon, Oscar and other relatives gathered and began to build the cottage which my mother named Sleepy Hollow. For 65 years, until my mother died in 1997, our family enjoyed our little bit of Little Harbor, spending time on weekends, launching our boat, fishing, camping with friends, and entertaining groups of relatives and friends from church. Because of state regulations, I was forced to sell the cottage upon my mother's death. But I still have a few stones from the beach of Sleepy Hollow sitting here on my desk— memories of 65 wonderful years in Little Harbor.

The cottage played a big part in all of our lives. We spent almost every Sunday afternoon there. We entertained guests there, we had church youth group meetings there, sometimes I spent several days there. My dad, Norm and I went together to buy a boat. It was a Larson, made in Peshtigo, right across the waters of Green Bay. Larson was a premier boat builder back then, and the boat, 15 feet long and made of cedar strips, was shipped to Sturgeon Bay by train. We went down to the depot and loaded it off a flatbed railroad car onto our trailer and took it to the cottage. With our 15-horse Johnson motor, we really thought we had something. We took lots of boat rides, used it for fishing, and went swimming from it. My dad seldom rode in the boat except for fishing. But when anything went wrong with the motor, he was right there to fix it.

Sometimes a friend and I would walk out to the cottage, seven miles, and then stay there overnight. Often my dad and I would go out there on a Saturday, and he always let me drive out there and back. In fact, that is the only place I drove until I got my license. So when I turned

15, he took me out to the county shop. The man asked if I could drive. My dad said yes. So I gave him my birth date and $2 and I had my first driver's license.

For me, the cottage was not only a place for fun, a place to entertain our friends and guests, but also a place of inspiration. The beauty, the silence, the wide expanse of the horizon over the water—all of that, along with my memories of playing with my friends in the sand down on the beach—I will never lose my fond memories of Sleepy Hollow.

3

MY DAD

When my dad left the farm and moved to Sturgeon Bay, he was an auto mechanic for many years, working at Moellers' Garage first, then later at another garage, Jackson's. When the Second World War began, Sturgeon Bay became a large shipbuilding town, building boats for the Navy. So Dad got a job at Peterson Builders, where he became foreman of the machine shop. When boats were launched, there was a ceremonial breaking of a bottle of wine as the boat went into the water for the first time. They began with the wife of the owner, Fred Peterson, then the wives of his two sons, then of other important people. Finally it got down to the wives of the foremen. So one boat was launched by my mother. It was a huge event, and they made quite a day of it.

One time Peterson's was building a boat that had to be delivered to New Orleans. My dad thought there was a chance that he could go on that trip as a crew member, and he thought that maybe he could get me on as cabin boy. It would have been loads of fun, boating down the Mississippi River, but unfortunately it never came off.

As foreman of the machine shop, some evenings my dad had to work overtime. When that happened my mother would pack a lunch, and I would take it down to my dad on my bicycle. Since the shipyard was building ships for the Navy, the whole building was protected by government security people. So I would go down there, talk my way in, and deliver Dad's lunch in the shop. After the war was over and there were no more ships to build, Peterson Boat Works shut down, so my father had no job. But we were close to Dr. Dan Dorchester, and Norm was working for him, so my dad got a job as custodian at the Dorchester and Beck Clinic.

One year, my dad took me deer hunting in northwestern Wisconsin. With three other men, we lived in a small camper, so small that I slept on the floor. We camped near a little stream, which we used for everything, drinking, washing our dishes, brushing our teeth. Water was different in those days.

One morning, a light snow had fallen, and I thought I saw deer tracks in the snow. I began following it, getting further and further away from our camp. And the wind had blown the snow, and I could no longer tell where the tracks were going. As I looked around, I had no idea where I was. My dad always wore a whistle around his neck, and he had given me one to wear also. So I blew my whistle as loud as I could, and nothing. No response. I began walking, though I had no idea where our camp was. I saw a power line, but I didn't know on which side of the line I should be. So I walked, and every five minutes I would blow my whistle. Nothing. After I had walked in the woods almost an hour, I blew my whistle good and loud, and I heard another whistle. I hurried off as fast as I could towards where the whistle noise came from, and suddenly, there in a small clearing in the woods, was my dad, standing on a small stump. He had come after me to rescue me.

One day when my dad was over at his brother Oscar's home he saw, stuck in a garbage barrel, part of a .22 rifle. He retrieved it, brought it home and gave it to me. I found somebody who could repair it and replace the missing parts. So I had myself a .22 rifle. In the back of the cottage was a huge bluff. I would go halfway up the bluff with some tin cans and set them on a ledge. Then I would go back to the cottage and from there, pick off those cans.

My dad was an Elder of the Sturgeon Bay Moravian Church for many years. He was the Sunday School treasurer for 25 years. When he brought the money home he let me go through it to find Indian-head pennies. I found 30 or 40 through the years. One day one of the members of the church told me that his small son thought my dad was Jesus. "Why is that?" I asked. "Because they always sing a song, 'Pennies for Jesus,' and your dad came by each Sunday to pick up the offering."

Down by the swimming beach was a small island, and on that island, living with her father, was a woman who was crippled and unable to walk at all. In those days, I don't think there was anything like a wheelchair, so she moved by skidding on the floor and hopping, using her hands to move. She was a member of the Moravian Church, so very often on Sunday we would drive down there, and my dad would pick her up and carry her to the car. Then we would stop at the home of the man who printed the church bulletins, and I would sit in the back seat of the car and fold the bulletins as we drove to church.

My dad was working at the Dorchester and Beck Clinic as custodian when I was about to graduate from Seminary. He had bought a new, used car so he could drive out to Bethlehem for that. However, one day at work, he found himself not feeling well, so he lay down on a sofa in the clinic waiting room. Dr. Dan walked by and saw him, and immediately took him to the hospital. But before they got there, my dad had died of a heart attack. This was on the Saturday before Easter, 1951. I immediately took a train to be home for the funeral. He died at the age of 60. His birthday was July 6, the same birthday as John Hus.

MY MOM

My mother was the best mother anyone could want to have. She was kind, generous, always helping others. She kept her family clothed, fed, healthy and happy. She entertained a lot at the cottage, and she enjoyed every minute of it. She often had a crowd of 12 or 15 around the table, and her favorite food was Swedish meatballs. Besides her sewing skills, she was also a barber, cutting hair for me and Norm, for my dad, for her dad Hans, and often for cousins who would ask her to cut their hair.

She was also a dentist. In those days, it was customary for children's teeth to be extracted as soon as they were loose. So my mother pulled teeth for me and Norm, but also for all our cousins. She would tie a thread around the loose tooth, give it a yank, and the tooth was out. When a person died in the presence of the family, she was the one who took charge. She knew how to take care of arrangements and comfort the family.

In those days the train still came to Sturgeon Bay, and with it the bums riding on the freight cars. Often they would stop at our house and ask for food. My mother always made them a sandwich and let them sit on the front porch to eat it. My grandfather and grandmother,

Hans and Anna, lived down on Cedar Street, now 3rd Avenue, and when my grandmother got sick and could no longer care for herself, we moved from our home on Leonhardt Street down to their home on Cedar Street so my mother could take care of both of them. We lived with them for five years, until my grandmother died. Then we moved back to our own house, taking my grandfather to live with us, and we also gave a room to Aunt Annie, as she no longer had the room with her folks.

For quite a few years after my father's death, my mother and Norman lived together in our home, but after Norman died in 1989 she could no longer live by herself. So we had a bedroom, bath and closet finished in the basement of our home in Chaska, and she lived there with us for only nine months. Then she had to go to a nursing home in Shakopee, Friendship Manor, where she lived for seven years. Fortunately I was working at the food shelf in Shakopee, so I was able to visit her almost every day. We celebrated her birthdays, Christmas, and other holidays with her. She passed away in 1997 at the age of 103 after a long, successful, happy life, being loved by all who knew her.

CHAPTER 5

MY BROTHER NORM

My brother Norman was born in 1920, so he was seven years older than I was. For this reason we were never in competition with each other. Instead I looked at him as my mentor. He also was my Boy Scout Scoutmaster for five years. Even yet, a day seldom goes by that I don't do something and then remember that Norm taught me how to do that: electricity, woodworking (he showed me how to safely use a table saw, and now his table saw is mine in our garage), leatherworking, chemistry, first aid, ropes and knots, setting up a tent and camping, using a boat motor, fixing things, and so many other things that I learned from him.

When I was 7, and Norm was 14, he was diagnosed with diabetes (there were no type 1 or type 2 in those days). This was in 1934. Insulin had just been developed by Eli Lilly in 1923, so it was brand new on the market, and fairly crude in its delivery system. Three times a day, before each meal, Norm would get a bottle from the basement steps (we did not have a refrigerator yet), put a new needle on his syringe, fill the syringe from the bottle, put the syringe in a gun, and inject himself with insulin. As a 7-year-old, I watched with curiosity, but sure that would never be me. We bought a gram scale so my mother could weigh every gram of food he ate, and we were introduced to some new vegetables, broccoli and cauliflower, and a new sweetener, saccharine.

This was long before the time of meters and strips. You tested for sugar in the urine by putting some urine in a test tube, adding a chemical indicator, and heating it over a Bunsen burner. When it changed color, you compared it with a color chart, and that told you your blood-sugar level. Since labs were few and far between, our family doctor, Dr. Dan, showed Norm, now in high school, how to test urine, which he did for himself. But Dr. Dan had other patients who were not able to do this type of testing. So he hired Norm to come to the hospital a couple of times a week (we lived only three blocks away) and test the urine for his other patients. From this elementary introduction to lab testing, after high school Norm enrolled in a nine-month course in medical technology at the Northwest Institute of Medical Technology in Minneapolis, and he became a certified lab technician.

After some time, Norm set up a new lab for Dr. Dan, and they eventually hired two lab techs to be supervised by Norm. Together, they did the lab work for the entire county.

During those early years, no one knew exactly how to control the effects of insulin, so sugar lows were a fairly common occurrence. Norm and I slept in the same room, and how I remember those mornings when, before it was time to get up I would hear Norm moaning in bed, suffering from a sugar low. I would call my parents and they would immediately call Dr. Dan, who would quickly come to our house and give Norm an injection of glucagon, and Norm would quickly pull out of the sugar low. One time we were at Chetek, living in the same cabin when, early in the morning, he had a low. His moaning frightened the other campers. Finally we found a doctor in town who was willing to come out to camp and give Norm an injection. How fortunate that, in those days, doctors were willing to make house calls.

Because of my mother's constant oversight of what he was eating, and of his own determination to live a good life in spite of diabetes, Norm went on to become a high school teacher.

Stout Institute, now University of Wisconsin-Stout, was a school in Menomonie, Wisconsin. At that time they had only two majors: Home Ec for the girls and shop, Industrial Arts, for the boys. So Norm went there for four years studying shop. After becoming a certified teacher, he taught in three or four smaller towns around Wisconsin, and then he got a job at Sevastopol.

Now he could live at home with my mother and they could care for each other. After he had taught a few years at Sevastopol, he finally retired. He kept busy working with the Scouts, making furniture for church, fixing things around the house, and taking care of our mother who, more and more, was needing someone to look after her. Living with diabetes, he did well to reach the age of 69, which he was when he died of a heart attack.

CHAPTER
6

SCHOOL DAYS

I went to school—kindergarten, elementary and high school—all in the same building. So I spent more hours of my life in that building than any other place until Chaska. And about a dozen of the kids who were with me in kindergarten also graduated from high school with me. There was one classroom for each grade, with 25 or 30 in each class, so it was very convenient that way. School was about five blocks from my home, and we all walked to school—no buses in town. On my way there was one house that had a bulldog, and I was deathly afraid of it. So my mother, while I was in kindergarten, walked me to school every morning and came to get me every day when school was over.

In kindergarten there were no desks. Instead we sat on the floor in a circle, sitting on pillows or rugs that each person had brought. I had a rug my mother had woven, and it was longer than it was wide. So whenever a visitor came and had no rug, that person sat on my rug with me.

While I was in kindergarten, the high school was putting on a play, which they did a couple of times each year. In one play, they needed a "little Dutch boy with a wooden shoe" at Christmastime, and he had to skip

around with his older sister. I was selected to be that boy, but I had to learn how to skip. So after class, my kindergarten teacher taught me how to skip, and I was in the high school play.

In all my classes from grades one to seven, my teachers were all old ladies with gray hair. I got along with them all and got good grades, but they weren't much fun. But in eighth grade, we finally had a younger, rather good-looking, teacher who dressed well. I got along well with her. In fact, once a month, she would call me up to her desk and give me her paycheck. I would walk downtown to the Bank of Sturgeon Bay and cash her check, and then walk back to school and give her the money. So I liked her a lot.

When I got to high school there were a lot more kids, because now the kids from the Catholic school joined us, as they had no high school. And the country kids, who had gone to their small country schools, now were bused into town for high school. So there were a lot more kids and more classes. Mr. Steinhoff was the science teacher—general science, physics and chemistry—and he also was the band director. I got along well with him and did well in his classes, so well that I was asked to tutor some of the students who couldn't quite understand science. So instead of going to study hall, I would often go to the library and tutor some of the other kids.

We walked home for lunch, and then back to school again for the afternoon. We couldn't get into the building until five minutes to 1. But Mr. Steinhoff gave me a pass so I could get in early, and I would go to the science storeroom and clean and straighten up the room. If there were two half-bottles of some chemical, I would put them together, and I would generally clean and organize things in the room.

Mr. Steinhoff also gave me my own key to the band room. There were two reasons for that. Besides the other percussion instruments—bass drum, snare drum and other things—I played the timpani. Now timpani you had to tune before each use, and that took a little time. You had to tune each turn screw separately, and you did that by gently snapping the drumhead by each one, and then while listening very carefully tightening or loosening the screw to get it in tune. With my own key, I could go into the bandroom early and get my drums tuned by the time rehearsal was to begin. Also, it seemed that I was the only one who could replace a broken drumhead. Often the orchestra director would come to my study hall and get me out to go to the bandroom and tuck a head. In those days new drumheads came as a rolled-up piece of sheepskin. You had to soak the skin in water overnight, and then you had a tool with which you had to tuck the skin under and around the rim, nice and tight, so that when it dried it would be tight and even all around. Today new drumheads come already tucked on a new rim, but in those days you yourself had to tuck it on the rim. So that was another reason I needed my own bandroom key. Also, when Mr. Steinhoff was there with me, he often would help me with my algebra.

The orchestra director just begged me to be in his pit orchestra to play at the high school plays. I was the only one who could play the timpani as well as the other percussion instruments, so I agreed to play for him in the pit. That way I got to see all of the plays numerous times.

I only took one semester of typing, on an old Royal manual. But that seemed to do it for me, and it has lasted my whole life through. I liked the typing teacher a lot, and when I didn't have my bike, I would walk home with her. I also had an "in" with another teacher. While working at Pleck's, I got to know quite well one of the girls, ladies, in the office. She lived just four houses away from our house. Well, Gen quit Pleck's to teach Home Ec in the high school. Now in those days, Home Ec was only for girls, so I couldn't take her class. But she was still my friend. So I took a bunch of small pieces of paper, stapled them together, and she signed each one on the bottom. So whenever I needed a pass for something, I could just write what I needed on the slip and it was already signed by a teacher. I even rode her home on my bike one day. She sat on the top bar of the bicycle frame in front of me, and we had a good time.

As I approached the end of my fourth year in high school, it worked out that I had to be in Bethlehem to begin college a few weeks before high school was over. (I was beginning college with the summer semester.) So I went to the principal and told her that I would have to leave high school three weeks early. She said I could just go to each of my teachers and take an oral exam to pass the class. Well, I went to each of the teachers, but we just visited. I told them my plans, and none of them had me take an oral exam, they just said I was good to go. So on the night of my graduation I had already been in college three weeks, and Norm walked across the stage and got my diploma.

So, all in all, high school was a fun time. I learned what I needed to, I did a lot of growing up, and I graduated somewhere in the top ten in my class, a class of maybe 150 students.

CHAPTER
7

THE DOOR COUNTY FAIR

When I was young, one of the highlights of my summer was the Door County Fair. It was held at the fairgrounds just north of Sturgeon Bay. It was a highlight because of my responsibilities there. Our Boy Scout Troop had been asked by the Fair Board to handle two things: the first aid station and the messenger service. So we set up our campsite between the entrance and the Fair Board office. We had a rope fence around the site. with a large arch built of small logs and tree branches with a sign, "First Aid Station." Remember, this was in the early 1930s, and there were no EMTs or ambulances at every corner. And we Boy Scouts had been well trained in first aid. We even entered teams in first aid competitions, going to Green Bay and other places. I had been trained by Doctor Dan Dorchester, our family doctor, and his was the office in which both Norm and my dad worked. In some of the advanced classes I was the only young person, so Dr. Dan always used me to give demonstrations on—to show how to bandage my arm or how to give artificial respiration. Norm went on to take some additional classes which I couldn't take, and he became a certified Red Cross first aid instructor. He gave classes in many towns up and down the peninsula—Ephraim, Fish Creek and others.

So I felt qualified to be the first aid person at the fair. I knew how to use smelling salts when a person had fainted or felt faint. I could take care of a wound by covering it with either iodine or something called Mercurochrome. Then, if it wasn't bleeding, we would not cover it with a bandage because the open air would help in the healing. And I knew when carrying someone on a stretcher, you carried him feet first so you wouldn't hit his head as you walked. And we all knew how to do artificial respiration when someone had drowned or was electrocuted and was not breathing and had no pulse. You had the patient lie on his back, and you straddled him, then you pushed his ribs in and up from the side, about once a second. Again, there were no CPR or external defibrillators hanging on the wall. So we did first aid as we knew it.

Then our other responsibility to the Fair Board was to act as their messenger service. There was only one phone line into the fair, and it was in the office of the Fair Board. So if they had to contact someone who perhaps was over by the grandstand, they would call us and give us the message, and we would run out to find the person who needed to be contacted. Again, this was about 60 years before the cell phone was invented.

In our campsite, we had a larger wall tent with a cot and our first aid supplies, and then we had a few pup tents we slept in overnight. So we could enjoy the fair all day long. We got to know the operator of the Tilt-A-Whirl, my favorite ride. And if we would give him a couple bottles of chocolate milk, he would let us ride on the Tilt-A-Whirl free and as long as we wanted to. So the fair was a lot of fun for us. (Years earlier, Norm played the guitar and mouth organ, and I sang, so we entered the amateur contest. We won third prize for $10.00. I was about seven at the time.)

So after that, I still enjoy going to fairs, walking around, taking a ride or two and playing some of the games.

(What do you call a big, round wheel that goes around at a fair or amusement park and it's made of iron? A ferrous wheel, of course.)

CHAPTER
8

BOY SCOUTS

From the time I was 12 until I became 17, I was a Boy Scout, and my scoutmaster was my brother Norm. We took our tents and went camping many times. We camped at the Potawatomi Park in Sturgeon Bay, at the Peninsula State Park in Fish Creek, at the scout cabin on the shore of Lake Michigan, in Green Bay, and other places. This meant setting up a tent, keeping dry in a tent, cooking meals, studying nature. Sometimes we were by ourselves, but other times we were at a camping program with many other troops. Then you had contests with the other troops—contests n first aid, in tying knots, in building a camp fire, and in making a fire using fire by friction. This meant you had a board of yucca wood, made a small hole in it, then you used a spindle that was turned by a bow. As that spindle in the hole got hot, a spark would form. You dropped that spark in some dry tinder, blew it and, if you were lucky, it would flame up. The contest was to see who could produce a flame in the shortest time. Well, with Norm's help, I got this down to a science. I had dry, dry yucca wood for the board and the spindle. On the top end of the spindle, which I held in my hand, I had a set of ball bearings. And my tinder was shredded cedar bark, several years old, and it had been in my mother's oven drying all day. So at the fire-by-friction competition, I could come up with a flame in about ten seconds. Most of the other boys never did get a flame.

As for camping equipment, we had my mother. She could make tents for us out of flour bags. When we needed knapsacks, she made them for us. This was years before backpacks became so popular. Back then, the only ones who used them were Boy Scouts. And she made bags and covers—if we could draw a picture of it, she could sew it.

When I got out to Bethlehem, I was Assistant Scoutmaster for the troop at the West Side Moravian Church.

CHAPTER 9

MAKING THINGS

I always liked to make things. We used to make our own kites. There was an open field at the end of our block, with no homes and no wires, so it was the perfect place to fly kites. We would get the kite high up in the air and then, when it was dinnertime, tie it to a stake in the ground. When we came back after lunch, it was still flying. Then we learned how to make parachutes. All we needed was a napkin, a couple of paper clips for weight, and a wire hook. You would hook the parachute to the kite string, shake it a little bit, and the wind would blow it up the string to the kite. Then you would shake the string and the parachute would be released and slowly sail to the ground.

I wanted to have my radio wake me in the morning instead of a noisy alarm clock. This was long before Westinghouse and GE were making radio alarm clocks, so I made my own. I made a wooden box, screwed a windup alarm clock to the bottom of it, and above it put a shelf with a hole in it. On the shelf I put a pull-chain switch, and plugged the radio into it. Then I tied the pull chain to the alarm winder on the clock. When it went off in the morning, the clock winder, as it went around, would pull on the switch chain, and lo and behold, music. Whenever we had clocks, radios, or other small units that were no longer usable, I would take them apart, just to see how they were made. I learned to use simple tools by doing this.

CHAPTER
10

PLECK'S DAIRY

"Particular people prefer Pleck's pasteurized pure perfect products." That's a phrase my cousin Kenny and I made up, long before I ever worked there. Pleck's Dairy was one of Sturgeon Bay's oldest and largest companies.

Louis Pleck was the sole owner of the business that had been started by his father years ago. Since it was the only milk bottler around, business was good. They bottled milk which was pasteurized and homogenized, cream, chocolate milk, butter, cottage cheese, and ice cream. Then they also bottled PepsiCola and their own line of flavored sodas. So everyone in Door County knew the Pleck's name, and everyone also depended on their products.

Now they had two kinds of quart glass bottles. The blue ones were route bottles. People got milk in them and returned the empties. But the milk sold in stores was in red bottles, with a nickel deposit on them, so that they would get the bottles back to the store. One day, when I was about ten years old, I was walking home and a house a block away was having an auction sale. I watched a little while and the auctioneer had a box of milk bottles—you couldn't see how many, but several.

I bid a dime on it and the auctioneer smiled and said, "Sold." I took the bottles home and washed them, then separated them, and I had seven store bottles, the red ones worth a nickel. So I walked down to Pleck's, and my later friend Gen gave me 35 cents for them. While I was doing that, Louie Pleck came walking down the stairs. I told him I had bought these bottles at an auction sale. He said, "I hope you didn't pay too much for them." No, I said, only a dime. That was my first introduction to Louis Pleck, whom I would see a lot of during my nine years working there.

When I was in high school, I thought I should get a job. Now I was already known by the people there at Pleck's. The manager, Delbert Newton, was a Moravian, so he knew me from church. And my Uncle Ole, father of Howard, Vernon, Don and Jeanne, was in charge of the back room — the drivers, the trucks and the product they took out.

So I went down to Pleck's to talk to Newt. Yes, he would hire me effective immediately. But I had one problem: after two weeks Chetek was to begin, and I wanted to go to Chetek. "No problem," said Newt. He agreed to pay me right through the week of Chetek, and I could work extra hours to make up for that week.

I was only 15, but I now had a job, so I had to get a Social Security card so they could "deduct from my pay to pay Social Security." My first job there was to be the bell boy. When a customer came into the office to get something, the girls there would press a button which would ring a bell out in the plant. I would poke my head out the door and see what the customer wanted. Milk, chocolate milk, butter, or pop. Then I would go and get the order, bag it and bring it into the front office. If it was a case of pop, I would carry that out to their car. Then I learned to wash milk bottles in a machine. There were no paper cartons then, or gallons. All milk was sold in glass one-quart bottles.

And I learned to wash 10-gallon milk cans. There was no refrigeration for bulk milk on the farms; they just put the milk in 10-gallon cans, and tried to keep them cool. For many farmers, a truck would come by and pick up the milk, and bring in milk from 20 to 25 farmers. We would empty the cans from each farmer, weigh the milk, test the milk for butterfat content, then wash the cans in a machine and return the cans to the truck, which would bring the cans back to the farmer the next day. Other farmers would bring in their own milk each day.

Then we would pasteurize the milk. That meant heating to a certain temperature and holding it there for so long. While I was there, the homogenizing process was discovered. That meant mixing the milk so much that the cream no longer would rise to the top of the bottle. So then we sold two kinds of milk, just pasteurized or pasteurized and homogenized.

When I began there the milk was bottled in a simple machine. Milk ran through a pipe into a tank above the bottling machine. The lead person would take two bottles out of a case of 12 bottles and hold them under the spout to fill, and then the bottles moved on to be capped. Then the assistant would take those two bottles and put them in an empty case. Often I worked as the assistant. But our main man who bottled milk had epilepsy. He could not get a driver's license, so he rode a bike to work. Once a month, almost like clockwork, he would have a seizure, fall to the ground, wave his arms around, make odd sounds. Newt knew how to handle this. We moved him into the butter room, watching that he didn't bite his tongue. When it was over, in maybe half an hour, Newt would drive him home, and I would become the main bottler the rest of the day.

Later on, we got a new bottling machine where you put the clean bottles on a track; as they moved along they were filled and capped, and then someone just took them off and put them in a case.

When we made ice cream in cardboard cartons, pints and quarts, I would often be called on to close the lids of the cartons after they were filled.

Now Uncle Ole was in the back in charge of deliveries. So often when a motel or large store needed a special order, usually pop but sometimes milk products, Ole would call me back there, and I would take that product out to them in a pickup. I did a lot of special things like that for Ole. He had his other drivers to supervise. Some of them he caught stealing, either money or product. But he knew he could count on me. He had other drivers to watch, but I was always "his sister's boy."

We wore rubber boots all day long, as the floor was always wet. Then in the evening before going home, we washed down the floor with a hose and water. I fully enjoyed my work at Pleck's, and I stayed there for nine years, through high school, college and seminary, summers and vacation times, when they would call on me to work.

One day when my summer vacation from school had just begun, so I could now work full time, Newt approached me. We had one guy, Arnie, who had been the retail, house-to-house delivery driver, the classic milkman. Arnie had done that for many, many years. But now he had given Newt notice that he was leaving. So Newt asked me if I would like to take over that route. He would pay me $25 a week for the route, working from 4 in the morning until noon; then, after lunch, I could work the afternoon and get paid by the hour. It didn't take long before I said yes. When I told my mother that my new job started at 4 in the morning, she was flabbergasted. How would I ever be able to get up and be at work by 4 a.m.? So for the next week, I rode along with Arnie to learn the routes. There was the Monday, Wednesday and Friday route and the Tuesday, Thursday and Saturday route. After a week of learning, Arnie was gone and I was on my own.

This is how it worked: I got up early, walked to work (only four blocks), opened up the plant at 4 a.m., got out my panel truck, gassed it up and backed it up to the side door. The Sturgeon Bay cops, the night crew, were always looking for something to do, so they came in almost every morning. I gave them a couple bottles of chocolate milk, which they drank as I was loading my truck. I loaded around 70 cases of milk, 12 bottles to a case, and took off. I learned to hold 12 one-quart milk bottles in my hands and arms, so I wouldn't have to make two trips for the empties. About 7 o'clock I would return for another load, and then about 10 o'clock I came in for a third load.

A couple of things happened while on that route. One morning I unlocked the door and right away I smelled ammonia leaking from the refrigerant in the coolers. It was filling the whole plant, so I couldn't go in because you couldn't breathe. Well, I needed to get my milk out, so I got out my truck and drove down to the fire station. I knew there would be somebody awake there all night, so I borrowed their gas mask. Wearing that, I could go into the plant, get out my milk, return the gas mask to them and be on my way. By the time I got back for my second load, Newt had been there and aired the place out.

One lady on my route owned a cherry orchard. Every day during cherry season, she put out with her empty bottles a bag of cherries for me.

One of the prominent doctors in town was Dr. Beck, the partner of Dr. Dorchester, our family doctor and in whose clinic Norm worked as a Med Tech, and where my dad was working when he died. I got to deliver milk to Dr. Beck's house around 10 each morning. Always waiting to meet me were his two children, little Johnnie and his younger sister. Well, that little Johnnie also grew up to be a doctor in Sturgeon Bay like his father. But I don't think he remembered that milkman he always waited for.

Sometimes I would have to work on Sundays. The choir in church was directed by my best friend, and I always sang in his choir. So when I had to work Sunday morning I would pull up my truck to the church side door, run in, put a choir robe over my stripped coveralls, be in church until the choir anthem, sing the anthem, then leave through a side door, rip off the robe, and run out to my truck.

We had a book with one page for each customer. There were a couple hundred pages. We were supposed to write down each customer's order as we delivered it. Well, that took way too much time. So I would deliver the whole route, then park somewhere under a shade tree and fill out the book. I tried to remember when someone got more than their regular order, and I don't think I missed too many.

Finished by around noon, I put my truck away and had lunch. I didn't very often go home for lunch. Just across the alley from the plant was a little restaurant that served a delicious brisket at noon. I got to know the lady who owned the place and also was the cook. So I would go across the alley, go in the back door through the kitchen, find a chair and table, and she would take care of me. Then, about 1 o'clock, I would go back to the plant, put on my boots and my apron, and go to work in the plant.

The next summer, when I was 17, right after summer vacation began and I could work full time, Newt called me aside. Would I like to drive the milk truck up north every day, to deliver bottled milk to all the stores, restaurants, motels and hotels. All of these places had enough inside refrigeration to hold enough milk for the winter population. But when summer came, the population grew to thousands; with all the summer visitors, they did not have nearly enough refrigeration. So we solved their problem by getting a bunch of yellow barrels. We would pack 27 one-quart bottles of milk in each tub, then shovel it full of ice and cover it with a canvas cover. When we delivered the milk in iced barrels, they could be left outside in the shade, and the merchants could bring in milk as they needed it.

So of course I took the job. I was now 17. The first thing each morning, I would take a pickup to the ice house. In winter, men had cut ice in the bay when it was frozen over, in chunks maybe 2 feet by 2 by 3. They were heavy. But I would load maybe 15 chunks of ice in the pickup, drive to the plant, and slide them down a chute to the basement. Then I would chip the ice into smaller pieces and throw them in a crusher, which loaded them onto a belt which took the ice up to the plant. Then we would shovel ice into each barrel. I suppose I needed 125 barrels each day. We loaded them onto a stake truck with an oversized bed.

Before we left, my helper and I would get some Pepsi-Cola for the trip. I never worked in the pop bottling part, but it was right there. So we would take a bottle off the line after it had gotten a shot of syrup, but before it got the carbonated water. Then we would put the bottle back in the line to get another shot of syrup, then the water, and take it out before it was capped. That was real Pepsi-Cola, believe me. I then brought milk to all the towns up north: Jackson Port, Bailey's Harbor, Fish Creek, Ephraim, Sister Bay, Ellison Bay, and Gills Rock. We took care of every store, restaurant, motel and hotel in the northern part of Door County. In those days most people paid cash, so I would write out a ticket and collect their money. Only a few of the larger places used credit. At the end of the day, if we had milk left, we would stop at some of the larger accounts and give them a couple of extra barrels of milk, so we never brought any milk back. Sometimes at stores we would run into the man who was delivering donuts, so we would trade a couple of bottles of chocolate milk for a couple packs of donuts.

At that time, the minister of the Sister Bay Moravian Church was Warren Sautebin, a longtime good friend. The church was a few miles out of town, and the parsonage was next to the church. Often I would drive out there and put a couple bottles of milk and some chocolate milk on their front doorstep. They knew who it was from.

One day I was really sick and could not go to work. So Newt came to our house, right up to my bedroom, so I could tell him what was to happen on my route that day and what certain accounts wanted, so he could tell the person who was to take over for me that day.

I had a helper who was a classmate from high school, so we knew each other well. He was studying to be a Catholic priest. Inside the Peninsula Park, just outside of Fish Creek, was a girls' camp which we delivered to. One day on the way home, I said to Bob, "Why don't we invite a couple of girls from the camp to go with us on a double date?" Bob said, "I don't think I had better do that."

We would always get back to Sturgeon Bay around 8 o'clock in the evening or later. The highway we came back on went right by Uncle Ole's house. So as we came into town, he was always sitting on his front porch with his family. When they saw us, he would drive down to the plant to check us in. We would unload the barrels full of empty bottles, I would turn over to him my money and my book of tickets for the day, and we would call it a day.

The next year, just as summer came and I could work full-time again, Newt again called me in. We had a refrigerated truck, just like a Schwan's truck, for hauling ice cream. The truck was plugged into an electrical line to keep the refrigeration running at night. During the day the refrigeration ran off the truck motor. This truck delivered ice cream products to the same accounts as I had brought milk to the previous year. Again I said yes and had a very enjoyable summer. This summer my cousin, Norbert Lenius, was my helper. The truck had various compartments, all of them kept cold. We filled them with ice cream in various flavors in metal pails, either 2-1/2 gallons or 5 gallons. (Cardboard disposable pails had not yet been invented.) Then we had ice cream bars, Cheerios, and Drum Sticks. And we had ice cream packed in pint and quart cartons.

Again, Norby and I had a great summer. We got to know lots of the owners, and often they would invite us to have dinner with them, eating in their kitchen. We usually put the ice cream right in their coolers.

The drive home at night would take maybe 45 minutes, so to pass the time, we found snacks. Up at Gills Rock, at the very top of the peninsula of Door County, there was a little shack that sold fish, and they smoked their own chubs. Chubs were small fish that they cleaned and cut out the big bones, then smoked them. So often for our ride home, we would buy a pound or two of smoked chubs, and they were delicious. Or sometimes during cherry season, we would stop at a stand and buy a couple pounds of Bing cherries. They were tasty, too. And if we couldn't find either of these, in the back of our refrigerated truck we always had a broken box of Drum Sticks. So we were never hungry when we got home.

This was my last summer at Pleck's, as I had to start going to churches for the summer. But one day while I was in seminary and living in Hamilton Hall, I had visitors. Newt and his wife were visiting Bethlehem, and they took time to surprise me by looking me up, and we went off to have dinner together! What a pleasant surprise that was.

CHAPTER 11

MORAVIAN COLLEGE AND SEMINARY

I spent six years in Bethlehem, three for college and three for seminary. For college, I did one summer semester in 1945, and then I graduated after only seven semesters. So I graduated in 1948. Bishop Mewaldt was instrumental in getting me in to Moravian. He helped me become a candidate for the ministry, meaning I would have a full, 7-year tuition scholarship paid for by the church.

So sometime in May of 1945, my parents drove me to Green Bay, where I got on the train, the Chicago and Northwestern (no longer in existence). In Chicago, I took either the Pennsylvania or the New York Central to Buffalo and from there, the Lehigh Valley to Bethlehem, where it continued on to New York. When I got to Bethlehem, Dean Hassler, dean of the college, met me at the station. We drove out to college in the school station wagon, the old type with classic wooden doors. He took me to Comenius Hall, took the elevator up to third floor, and showed me my room. I was to room with two other guys; one was Wil Behrend, who later became a bishop of the church. The other one was not a Moravian. We had two rooms, one for a bedroom and the other to study in.

Now let me explain something. My first semester at Moravian, there were only 13 students in the entire college. These were the war years, and all young men faced the draft unless you were a student for the ministry, or worked in a war-related factory, or were a farmer, teacher, or doctor. If you were not in one of these "essential" places, you were drafted into the Army. So there were only 13 of us, all studying for the ministry. This meant that many of the teachers had to be let go, and those few who remained had to teach classes not in their field. The coach taught world history, the math guy taught lots of things, and the science guy was a part-timer they brought in to help out. Many in the church wanted to close the college, but Dean Hassler and President Ray Haupert said no, and together they made it go. So my college experience was a little different than college days now. However, the next year, the war was over, and then with the G.I. Bill, which completely paid for college for veterans, our ranks rose to over 200.

So back to my first day there. After I was settled in, Dean Hassler called my cousin, Howard Nelson, to come over and take me to dinner. Howard was the brother of Vernon, Jeanne and Don Nelson. He was now in seminary and had one more semester to go. So he introduced me to Bethlehem. Incidentally, I followed Howard in serving the North Dakota churches, Goshen and Casselton. After six years there, he then went to Green Bay East, and I followed him in North Dakota. Sadly enough, Howard died while in Green Bay, the result of an appendix surgery.

I got along quite well in college. I didn't get real close to any of my teachers, as I did in high school. But Dean Hassler knew me, liked me and I was sort of special to him. Whenever prospective students and their parents came to visit the campus, Dean Hassler always asked me if he could show them my room — guess he knew it would always be presentable. And I got especially close to the President, Raymond Haupert. I guess if you're in with the administration, you don't have to worry about the teachers.

Dr. Raymond Haupert was a Moravian minister. He was a PhD, had a whole pile of degrees, had done archeological research in Israel, and was on the committee to translate the new Revised Standard Version of the Bible. He grew up in West Salem, where his father was the minister. His father then moved to Chaska, but Ray never really lived in Chaska, as he was in college by that time. When I was in West Salem, he and his wife came to visit me and see his old home town.

Dr. Haupert was fond of trains. He used to take his boys out to a railroad crossing just to see a certain train go by. In his desk drawer, he had a schedule for every train in America. He used to tell us, "If you have a speaking engagement out of town, you'd better take the train. If you fly, you'll never know when you are going to get there."

Well, somehow we got together, and he asked me to be his babysitter! He had four boys too young to stay alone, so I went out there when he and his wife, Estelle, would go out. Then I also helped him work on his lawn and yard. And one day I painted a part of his house. While in Seminary, if there was a problem — not enough heat, or something about our classes—I was the one delegated to go over to his office and get the matter settled.

Since the college was so small they couldn't offer a real wide variety of classes. So they offered beginning chemistry and physics. Well, I had learned them both quite well in high school, so I didn't have to study at all. At final exam time, I would lie on an upper bunk while the guys were cramming, and I would help them whenever they didn't understand something.

I don't think we ever had keys to lock our rooms; they were just left open. I used to have a few candy bars in my desk drawer. But often I would open the drawer and find some candy missing, but a quarter lying there! So I got an idea. I found a candy wholesaler not too far from college. I took my bike over to his house and bought six or eight boxes of candy bars. I put them on my desk with a little box for money, and the guys were quite glad for the service. Some days I'd find an IOU in the box, but they always paid it off. The school had no bookstore or snack bar of any kind, so this was the only food sold on the campus. Just before Christmas vacation, I sold dozens of boxes of chocolate-covered cherries. The guys wanted to take them home as gifts. One day I had another idea. Our baseball team was playing in a field near our house. A lot of spectators were there, standing as there were no bleachers. So I put together an assortment of candy bars and went over there and sold to the crowd. After doing this for a few days I was called by the college controller, who said, "You can't do that!" I asked why not, because I was not competing with anyone. But he shut me down on my outside sales, although I kept selling them in my dorm.

Looking around for work to earn a little money, I contacted the Coca-Cola company. They had a bottling operation in Bethlehem. After being practically weaned on Pepsi Cola, I now went over to the enemy—Coke. My job was working at supermarkets on weekends. They gave me a uniform to wear, with Coke insignia on it. In those days, the only way Coke came was in 6-1/2-ounce, green glass bottles. Canned pop had not yet been invented. These were packed in a 6-pack carrying case. So on an endcap, I would build up a huge display of these 6-packs of Coke. Then I had boxes of small lighters shaped like a Coke bottle. I learned how to open the lighter and light it with one hand, so I could be holding a 6-pack of Coke in the other. If the customer would let me put one 6-pack in her shopping cart, then I would sell her a Coke lighter for a quarter. In those days, lighters were much more popular than they are today, so I sold boxes and boxes of lighters. That was fun, and I sold lots and lots of Coke as well. However we did find an occasional 6-pack of Coke lying on the shelf with cookies or some other item. Guess some people wanted the lighter but not the Coke.

There was in Bethlehem an organization called Community Concerts. A group of people from the community would book four concerts: piano, small instrumental groups, singing groups, etc. Harry Belafonte was one group, only he wasn't with them. Then they would sell tickets all over town, and if they sold enough tickets so they had more money, they would book a fifth concert. For every ten tickets you sold, you got one ticket free. Well, I had a built-in audience in the dorms, so I sold about 40 tickets, more than any of the other sellers. So I got four free tickets, of which I sold two and kept two for myself.

During my early years in school, we had no book store, coffee shop, or anything like that. So there was no place to buy college stationery. Well, I got ahold of the college logo, took it to a printer and had him print up three reams of letterhead, and box of envelopes printed up with the return address, put them in packets of 20 letterheads and ten envelopes, and then I sold them at the school door to door. It wasn't long before I sold out.

But the best sales opportunity I had was selling all the seminary books. The seminary allowed one of the students to take care of getting all the books that students would need for their classes. Karl Bregenzer, a few years ahead of me, turned it over to me my last two years. I went to each professor and found out what books he would be using in his class and how many students would be in the class. Then I went to the publisher and ordered all the books the seminary would need for the year. I bought them for 60%, so I made a profit of 40% on each book. When the G.I. students were there I would just bill the government. Otherwise, the guys just bought them from me.

I made a few extra deals as well. There was a very well-known Bible encyclopedia called ISBE, the *International Standard Bible Encyclopedia*. It had five volumes, and it took over a foot of space on a shelf. It sold for $120.00. So I offered a bargain on the set, $75.00. It was a set that everybody would like to have, so I took orders, and got maybe ten orders. Then I ordered the books, and made out pretty well on that—and got a set for myself.

One of the first nights I was in Bethlehem, the youth

group from the West Side Moravian Church came out to college to meet us. We had a good time just sitting around on the grass outside, and of course they invited us to join them at West Side. There were at that time five Moravian churches in Bethlehem, and students could choose wherever they wanted to go. But this seemed like a nice group, and John Groenfeldt was the pastor. He was a Sturgeon Bay boy, so a bunch of us decided to go to that church. It was a very close-knit group. We guys tried to see that every girl in the group would have a date for Saturday night. One of our guys was a young Jewish boy who had escaped from the Nazis in Germany with a group of children who were taken from their families to England to be safe. Eventually he came to America, and when he heard about the Moravians, he enrolled in Moravian College. Well, there was one girl who needed a date, so I urged Ivan to call her, and I even gave him a nickel to call her with. Well, they had a date, then began going steady, and they ended up getting married. I still share Christmas cards with Ivan, and a few years ago they visited me in Chaska.

Our group was together several times each week: choir practice on Wednesday nights, then Sunday School, church, and most Sundays we were together for the afternoon to take a walk, go out to Illick's Mill for a wiener roast, or whatever. John Groenfeldt used to take some of us over to Camp Hope, the newly purchased campground which the Eastern District had bought, so we went over to work, cleaning up brush and working on the buildings before any camp programs were held there.

Often on a Sunday night, after our youth group

meeting at church, we went to someone's house. They all drank tea—no coffee at all. That is where I learned to drink tea and like it. And not just any tea—it had to be Constant Comment, a delicious tea flavored with orange rind. That's where I learned to love tea. Constant Comment is still sold today, and it's my favorite tea.

This West Side group was a valuable part of my experience in Bethlehem. A place to belong, places to go, things to do with kind, friendly people. Four of the girls, two at a time, came out west to go to Chetek. But before camp they all made a stop at Sturgeon Bay, where they stayed at my home for a few days. An unforgettable bunch of people, was the West Side group.

When it got to be May 1948, I had enough credits to graduate, but I had a problem. Two problems: I had only put in seven semesters, and you needed eight to graduate; and I did not have a major. When I began we were put in a Pretheolog Major. Then halfway through, they dropped this major and said we would get a Classics major. But because of scheduling conflicts, I did not get all the credits I needed for a Classics major. So I wrote two petitions to the faculty: one to let me graduate with only seven semesters and the other to let me graduate without a major. Then I hitchhiked home to Sturgeon Bay. My dad had just bought a new, used, car so I could drive both of them to Bethlehem for my graduation. They stayed at the home of one of the West Side girls. I gave them a grand tour of Bethlehem, and then after graduation I drove them to New York for a day and showed them the sights of the Big Apple. Then we drove home for my summer vacation. I graduated from college in 1948 with a B.A. and from seminary in 1951 with a B.Div. (Bachelor of Divinity). Then, a few years later, they changed our degree retroactively to Master of Divinity.

For those three years, all the seminary students who were not married lived together in a house on campus known as Hamilton Hall. There were maybe 12 of us living there. Then there were about eight married students who lived off campus.

I gained a lot during my six years in Bethlehem. I learned so much about being a Moravian, made many new friends, had many new experiences, learned much about the Bible and about religion. I value those years, as they gave me the inspiration to go out to the Church and be a pastor.

CHAPTER
12

MY YEARS IN THE PASTORAL MINISTRY

My brother Norman attended our church camp Chetek each summer. At that time, it was the only church camp in the Western District, for those ages 12 to 18. I could not wait until I was 12 so I could go with him. So I went when I was 12, and loved it. The next year, when I was 13, there was at Chetek a former missionary from Alaska. He spoke several times during the week, and he brought his kayak along and put it in the water by the swimming beach. We boys made a challenge to get into the kayak in chest-high water, without tipping it over. It was somewhat difficult to do, but I did it several times. But more importantly, his message of working in Alaska bringing the Gospel to the people there was of great interest to me, and I decided there that I wanted to be a missionary to Alaska.

That meant going to Moravian College and Seminary. So when school began that fall, I went to our principal and told her that I wanted to take the classes I would need to get into college. I was aware of this because my cousin, Howard, brother of Vernon, Don and Jeanne, was not able to get into Moravian without taking some high school classes the year after he graduated. And another friend of mine who applied to Moravian wanted to become a minister, but he was not accepted at all. Also, along the way I had to work with Bishop Mewaldt, who became a good friend through it, and with him apply to be accepted by the church as a ministerial candidate and get a full-tuition scholarship for seven years, both college and seminary. For that, I was required to serve at least ten years in the ministry, or I would have to pay it back. During my college years, the thought of going to Alaska as a missionary changed to becoming a pastor in the Western District.

CHAPTER 13

AURELIA, NORTH DAKOTA

Shortly before my senior year in college was over, I got a letter from Bishop Mewaldt asking if I would like to go serve our church in Aurelia, North Dakota, for the summer. In years gone by, Aurelia had been a successful functioning church when the farms in North Dakota were small, 80 or 160 acres, and there were enough people to make the church. The town of Aurelia was located northwest of Minot, N.D., close to the Canadian border. Earlier it had two grain elevators, a store, post office, railroad station that was staffed by a full-time agent and other businesses that made it a nice farm city. But when the farms began to get bigger and some families farmed eight or ten sections (with a section being one square mile), the population of the area fell dramatically. There were not enough people there to keep either the church or the town going. The one remaining store was also the post office and besides one grain elevator, that was all that remained. So the church closed, but the PEC (Provincial Elders' Conference, which provides executive leadership for the Moravian Church's Northern Province) decided to send a student out there during summers to keep the church going as well as they could. When I told Bishop Mewaldt that I would go out there the next summer, he sent me a letter, a license, that even though I was not ordained, I could serve Holy Communion. And you don't have to be ordained to do funerals. Of course, I could not do weddings, baptisms, or confirmations.

Since I did not have a car, I ordered a bicycle from the Spiegel catalog to be shipped right to Aurelia. I took the train out to Donnybrook, a little town just three miles from Aurelia. One of the men met me there. We stopped at a hardware store to buy a two-burner kerosene stove for me to cook on. There was no electricity in the church or parsonage, but I found two old gasoline lanterns. Neither one worked, but by taking parts from each one, I got one that worked. To keep food cold, there was a cistern that they filled with snow each winter. I had a rope with a bucket attached, so my Jello, butter, and milk I put in the bucket and lowered it into the cistern where there was still snow. Inside the house was an old-fashioned cistern pump. Each time you used it, you had to set aside a can of water that you needed to prime the pump next time you used it. If you forgot, you had to get some water from somewhere in order to use the pump again. The pump drained into a sink with a drain hole. Under the hole was a 5-gallon bucket. If you forgot to empty the bucket in time, you had a wet floor. So I took two pieces of 2 by 4, nailed them in an X with a piece of stiff wire leading up from the X. The wire I put through the drain hole in the sink, so as the bucket filled with water, the wire rose up in the sink, so I knew when the bucket was full and time to be emptied. And I had my new kerosene stove to cook on. In the outhouse out back was the Sears and Roebuck catalog that you used. Toilet paper had not yet made its way into the country.

I held Sunday services there each week, with about 40 in attendance. As was the old custom, in church the men sat on one side and the women on the other. The elevator operator was new to the area, and I invited him and his wife to come to church. He asked if they had to sit separately on both sides, but I assured him that he and his wife could sit together with no problem. We had an old pump organ in the church, and a woman who could play it. But when I came out there the second year, we now had electricity in the church and parsonage. So I hooked up one end of a hose to the organ bellows, cut a hole in the floor and ran the hose through it into the crawl space. In there, I hooked up a small blower attached to a sewing machine foot pedal. Then the organ worked 100% better.

Many Sundays I would be invited out to dinner with one of the families. But there was one dear couple who lived close to the church. They were the salt of the earth, and I spent a lot of time with them. The woman told me that any Sunday no one else invited me to dinner, I was welcome to eat with her family. Knowing that couple and feeling their love for me would have been enough to make the whole summer experience worthwhile.

The little store in town also was the post office. Each afternoon, the train came by, a single unit with both engine and passenger car in one. They didn't stop at Aurelia but they slowed down and threw out on the ground a bag containing the mail. And the outgoing mail was in a bag hanging close to the tracks, so a hook on the engine picked up that bag as it passed by. Every other Saturday, the store keeper and his wife had to go to Minot to get supplies. So those days, I became the store keeper and the Postmaster. I had to be sworn in as Postmaster. I kept the store open all day until around 5 o'clock, when the train would throw out the mailbag and I would walk down to the tracks and get the bag. Each family had a little cubbyhole, so I would sort the mail, putting each family's mail into their cubbyhole. Then they would have to come in to the store to get their mail. We had a gas pump out front. Near the top of the pump was a circular glass area with a scale for the number of gallons painted on it. You would pump gas to fill the container with the number of gallons they wanted, then gravity would run the gas into the car.

One of the farmers hired me to shock grain. It was so hot, over 100 degrees, so that I had to have a water jug at each end of the row! It was hot, hot, hot. When the day's work was over, they had a 55-gallon barrel filled with water, which would be heated by the sun. That was where you took your shower after work. Those people farmed seven sections.

The next summer I went out there again, only this year my folks had given me money to buy a car, so my second year was a little more comfortable. Then with electric lights, it was much easier to live there. A few years ago, seven of us who had been there as students had a reunion at Aurelia. When we went out there, the church, parsonage, and all the rest of the town was completely gone, the land now planted in wheat.

This was my introduction to the pastoral ministry, and I loved every minute of it.

14

GOSHEN AND CASSELTON, NORTH DAKOTA

Shortly before the end of my senior year in seminary, I received a letter from Bishop Mewaldt that was my official call to serve two churches in North Dakota, Goshen and Casselton. I had been at these churches before because my cousin, Howard Nelson, brother of Vernon, Don and Jeanne, was serving there. Several times on my way to Aurelia, I had stopped and stayed a few days with him. The parsonage was next to the Goshen Church, the larger church, about five miles from the town of Casselton and the smaller church. So I was happy now to have a job.

Graduation from seminary came, and I was ordained by Bishop Mewaldt on June 17, 1951, at Sturgeon Bay. The Sturgeon Bay church was planning to have a reception for me that included dinner and an afternoon program. But my cousin, Howard, who had just moved from Goshen and Casselton to the church in Green Bay East, had gotten sick and died. His funeral was on Saturday, the day just before I was ordained. So, since my whole family had been deeply involved in the funeral, they cancelled my reception. I didn't mind, as it was the right thing to do.

A week later, I drove out to Goshen to be the new pastor there. Each Sunday I had two services, Casselton at 8:30 and Goshen at 10:3C. Scme of the time I also had afternoon services at either our church at Alice when it was without a pastor, or at Embxden, about ten miles from Goshen. I served these churches for seven years. These people were again the salt of the earth, so kind, generous and thoughtful. At each annual church council, at which I presided, at the end they would ask me to excuse myself and go down in the basement while they voted on a bonus for me. Depending on their crops for the past year, they would decide how much to give me. It always was several hundred dollars.

One older man was especially fond of me. He came to the parsonage almost every day to see how we were doing, if we needed anything. Then often he and I would work on a church project fixing something, clearing the wooded area to make a picnic grounds, or something. His son was a prominent member of the church and his wife had us over for dinner almost every holiday, Christmas, Easter, Thanksgiving and others. So we felt we were really part of this family. The son had a yellow pickup truck. Often when I needed a pickup, I would borrow his and usually take his 5-year-old daughter with me.

While I was at Goshen we celebrated the 75th anniversary of the church. One of the members wrote a play which, for three evenings, we put on outside the church. We brought in bleechers from the high school, built a stage, had an old Model T Ford that you had to crank to get started. It was a major production, but they carried it off without a hitch. When I left there, I knew I left a lot of people who loved me.

THE DALE CARNEGIE COURSE

While I was at Goshen and Casselton, I was able to take the Dale Carnegie course in Fargo. Dale Carnegie wrote, in 1936, a book called *How to Win Friends and Influence People*. It was a massive best seller and remains popular today. Its themes were self-improvement, salesmanship, public speaking, memory, and interpersonal skills. He said some quotable things, like "Success is getting what you want. Happiness is wanting what you get." And "When fate hands you a lemon, make lemonade." And "Flaming enthusiasm, backed up by horse sense and persistence, is the quality that frequently makes for success." The popularity of the book led him to develop a course which tapped into the average American's desire to have more self-confidence. And public speaking was a huge part of that. When I got installed as pastor of Goshen and Casselton in North Dakota, I felt a need for some additional training in preaching and public speaking. So I wrote to the Dale Carnegie Company asking if their course was available in North Dakota. They responded that the course had never been taught in North Dakota, but they were negotiating with a man who was interested in setting one up. Before too long, I received an invitation to a dinner at a hotel in Fargo for anyone interested in the Dale Carnegie Course.

I called in to make reservations and attended. I was much impressed by the presentation, and even more impressed by the gentleman and his wife who presented the program. So I signed up for the once-a-week 16-week course. Each class ended with each person, about 30 participants, giving a 2-minute talk on some assigned topic. Then each member of the class voted for who had given the best talk. The winner was awarded a special mechanical pencil engraved with the Dale Carnegie logo.

I won the pencil for the ninth week, engraved with these words, Award for Best Sales Report. Then I also won the pencil at the final class, engraved with Highest Award for Achievement, Dale Carnegie Courses. I admired the instructor and his wife so much that we even had them out to the parsonage for dinner one evening.

After I moved to Wisconsin Rapids, I still kept in touch with my instructor and I thought it would be nice to become a professional instructor. But you had to take a long class, quite expensive, so I was not able to do that. However, they were going to begin a class in Wisconsin Rapids after I had moved there, and they asked me if I would like to be a volunteer instructor. I would teach the first hour and a half of the class each night and then the professional instructor, who would fly in just for the night, would teach the last half of the class. So I accepted. In my role I kept the class together each night, and I brought the supplies, awards and records. Then I would open the class, do the housekeeping things, and then give a lecture followed by a discussion of one of the topics the class covered. Then after a break, the professional would take over. Here each member would give a 2-minute speech on an assigned topic, and the instructor would critique the speech. Then the class would vote on who would win the pencil for the night. So for me, it was almost like going through the class again. All in all, I think my experiences with the Dale Carnegie classes had a deep and valuable influence on my life.

CHAPTER
16

KELLNER AND SARATOGA UNION, WISCONSIN RAPIDS, WISCONSIN

After around seven years at Goshen, I received a call from PEC to move to Wisconsin Rapids, Wisconsin, to serve two churches, Kellner and Saratoga Union. They had just built a new parsonage at Kellner; in fact, it was not quite finished when we moved in. Saratoga was not officially a Moravian Church, but it had been served by Moravian pastors its whole life long. The churches were about ten miles apart, so on Sundays, I held services at Saratoga at 9:00 and at Kellner, the larger church, at 11.

Warren Sautebin was the pastor at the Wisconsin Rapids Church, and we and our churches did many things together. We celebrated the 500th anniversary of the Moravian Church by renting the high school gym for a program. Also, we held an event for the completion of the new Revised Standard Version of the Bible. We combined our choirs and took them over to the Freedom Church to put on a concert. And we held a junior day camp together.

I got a bus driver's license, and we rented a bus for the week. I would first pick up kids at Kellner, then drive to Saratoga, then to the Rapids church to pick up the rest, and then drive out to a Girl Scout camp, Camp Sacajawea, hold our camp program, and then drive everybody back at the end of the day.

Also memorable from these days was the visit of Thor Johnson. Thor was the son of a former pastor at Saratoga, and he was a nationally known musician. He directed the Cleveland Symphony Orchestra and the Nashville Symphony. But at this time he was director of the Little Chicago Youth Orchestra. Well, they came to Wisconsin Rapids to do a concert. We invited Thor to come out to the Kellner parsonage after his concert. One of the ladies from Saratoga, Mabel, had been his babysitter while his father was pastor there, so we also invited her. Well, it was a great evening and at 3 o'clock in the morning, I drove Thor and Mabel home. I drove first to the Saratoga area to Mabel's home. When she got out of the car, Thor also got out and and planted a big kiss on the cheek of his former babysitter. Then I took Thor to his room in the hotel.

Two footnotes: First, while I was in Winston-Salem, we went to visit Thor's home. He was not at home, but his mother just beamed as she showed us Thor's room. Second, some time after that, I got a letter from Thor's father. He was now serving in the Southern Province. In the letter he said, "Al, you will never get anyplace serving churches in the Western District. Why don't you apply for a church in the Southern Province? The churches are much larger and you will have a much more successful ministry." I wrote to thank him, but I never took his suggestion seriously.

CHAPTER
17

WEST SALEM, ILLINOIS

After about five years at Kellner, I got another letter from the PEC. This was a call to serve the church in West Salem, Illinois. West Salem in located in the southeast corner of Illinois. People always asked, why is the town of West Salem in the east side of Illinois? The answer is that the founders of this town were Moravians from Winston-Salem. Their new settlement was west of Winston-Salem, so hence the name West Salem. When I accepted the call, I was told that this congregation needed to build an addition to the church, but none of the former pastors had been able to get them to move on it.

The West Salem church was a nice building, but there only was the sanctuary and the basement. The parsonage was across the street, and the church office was a bedroom on the first floor of the parsonage. They really needed space for an office, more Sunday School rooms, and a kitchen and fellowship hall. I talked to some people there about it, but at first, I didn't get much of a response.

Now this was the first time I had only one church to serve; however, they had services every Sunday morning,

Sunday evening, and every Wednesday evening. So I had to spend a lot of time getting sermons ready.

I became a member of the Rotary Club, and eventually was elected President. During that time, our local doctor, who also was a Rotarian, owned a piece of land on the main street, and he said he would donate that land and give money to build a library. The Rotary Club formed a library committee, of which I was the Chairman. I went and measured the lot so I knew how much land we were talking about, then I drew a floor plan for a library. I presented it to the committee, and they accepted it. So I hired a contractor, gave him my plans, and he built the library. Then we needed shelves, and I had built hundreds of shelves. So I drew up plans for all the shelves we needed, gave my plans to a carpenter, and he built them. Then we needed a card catalog, a holder with drawers, so I found and bought one, along with the cards, envelopes, and other library supplies. I bought some tables and chairs and a desk.

Soon the library was built, and we needed to dedicate it. So I put together a choir made up of members of the various churches, and picked out some music and rehearsed it with them. Then I got the mayor and a few politicians to speak, and I set up a dedication service held at the local gazebo on the town square. After the service, we had an open house at the library, along with refreshments.

At West Salem there was a large cemetery owned by the church. When the Moravians founded the town, they started a cemetery, and it became the town cemetery— except the Moravians had to take care of it. We needed the community to step up and help with the maintenance. One day one of the men gave me a thousand dollars which he said was for the cemetery. I said to him, "Buz, keep that money for now, and let me put together a fundraising campaign for the cemetery, and then you can give me the thousand." So I bought nine rolls of film — that was how we took pictures back then — and gave three rolls to two of my friends and told them to take pictures of anything in town, but use up the film in two weeks. Then I kept three rolls for myself. I took a lot of pictures of all the churches, the cemetery, and signs. Then I knew a guy who had a private plane, so I asked if he would take me up so I could take some pictures from the air. He was happy to, so we went up and I got lots of pictures, especially the church and the cemetery. When I collected all the pictures, I sat down and made a slide show, using only the best pictures. Then I planned a walking tour through the cemetery, and had a brochure printed up with the tour, step by step, and a lot of nice pictures of the cemetery.

Then I had the women put on a nice dinner, and I invited about 30 of the leading people of the community, people who had some wealth. After dinner, I showed the slide show, then handed out the tour brochure, then gave each one a folder with a pitch for the cemetery and an envelope. Before too long, I had collected ten thousand dollars. I talked to one of the members a few years ago, and he told me that by now, the fund had grown to several hundred thousand dollars, and they remembered that I had started that fund so many years ago.

My very best friend in West Salem was a young

man named John, who was manager of the local Ford garage. We spent a lot of time together and got to know each other quite well. One day I walked over to the shop, and entered by the back door as I always did. The first mechanic said to me, "Al, your car is in." I said, "What car?" I walked a little further and a second guy said to me, "Your new car is in." A little further and a third guy told me my new car was in. And before I got out of the shop, a fourth guy said the same thing. By this time I was at the office door, so I went in and said to John, "What's all this about my new car. I never ordered a new car." John said, "Well, Al, the Ford rep was in and he urged us to get in a station wagon. We said, 'Nobody around here buys station wagons. These people are all farmers, and they buy pickups and trucks.' He was rather insistent, so I said, 'Al is the only one around here who buys station wagons. Maybe we could sell one to him.' So Jim, the owner, and I, we picked out the colors we thought you would like, and equipped it with all the extras we thought you would want, and now the car is in." He showed it to me, and it was a nice car. They gave me a price, and the next day, Jim and I took it for a ride. We dickered a little bit. I asked for some more mirrors and floor pads. And I told Jim I would take it.

By now, there was more and more talk about a new addition. So the joint board and I went to visit some nearby new churches. And we began talking to some companies that built churches. We began working with one company whose deal was, for a price, they would give us blueprints of the building according to what we told them we wanted. Then we could buy and pay for the blueprints. If we wanted them to build the building, that would be in addition to what we paid for the blueprints. They gave us a price for the building, which we discussed at length. But one of the members on the board owned a lumberyard. Using the prints, he said he would work up a price. He did, and we signed a contract with him.

Now the church still had not voted officially to build. So we held a church council. On the motion to build, the vote was a tie. Normally with a tie vote, the person running the meeting, if he hasn't voted, casts the deciding vote. But I was not going to take that responsibility on myself, so I said we would call a meeting of the joint board, and they would decide how I should cast my vote. We had a meeting Monday night, and I didn't attend. But after an hour or so, two of the guys came over to the parsonage and said, "We voted to build!" So then we needed to have another fundraising campaign, which I organized. The campaign went well, money and pledges started to come in and then construction started.

I went over to see the work on the building every day. I knew the plans very well, as I had studied every nook and cranny. One day I was watching the workers lay pipe for the underground heating. I saw them laying the pipe straight, and I knew there needed to be a right angle there. So I told them, and they didn't believe me. I told them to go look at the plans and, of course, when they came back they had to change the pipes.

I studied every door in the building. Where on the wall should it be placed so as to get good traffic flow? On which side of the door should it swing? Should it swing in or out of the room? All these little details can make the building work well, or else things will be inconvenient. I wanted it to work well.

During all this, I received a call from the PEC to come to Chaska. They wanted me to come as soon as possible, and they said, "Come to Chaska and do the same thing." So the building in West Salem was finished, and I planned the dedication Sunday. I invited Rev. Dr. Ed Sawyer from Bethlehem to come out for the dedication. The next week I moved the office stuff from the office in the parsonage, but I never got to work out of there. The next Sunday was my farewell Sunday, and that week, I was off to Chaska.

West Salem was the kind of pastorate a minister can only dream of having. The people were so kind, so generous, so thoughtful, willing to follow my leading. I left many, many dear friends there. They were truly the salt of the earth.

A few weeks before I left, the Rotary Club, which really was the whole town, held a farewell dinner for me. After dinner they had a program, "This Is Your Life," which was based on a TV show that was popular at the time. At the end of the program, Doris, the wife of Jim Lear, the owner of the Ford garage, read a piece that she had written. It went like this:

ODE TO REV. LENIUS

Friends, Moravians, countrymen, lend me your ear,
I come to bring memories of one we hold dear
In years that will follow, we'll all have our share
Of thoughts of Rev. Lenius in the town on the square.
No cupful of coffee but rather of tea;
A Rotary meeting and its Presidency.

A ticket for speeding — the fault of the car;
Those choir rehearsals for concerts afar.
Then meetings with board members, working together,
And visits to sick folks in all kinds of weather.
A sore throat on Sunday that requires a glass of water,
That big day in August, with that soup we call "chowder,"
The study groups, Bible Schools, Sunday School classes,
A smile and "hello" to each person he passes.
The weddings, the funerals, the baptisms, too,
And camp at Tar Hollow — his work's never through.
A drive for the upkeep of the cemetery,
A drive for a building that seems necessary.
No shirking of duties, but giving of time,
A hope that the confirmand's progress in fine.
The music of spirituals — every sort;
Then a bowling party for those young-at-heart.
A license — AL (birthday???) one-four-five-seven;
And days that are filled up with kindness and giving.
No task was too large and no task was too small,
Because Rev. Lenius had time for all.
A church needs a minister, an earthly guide,
And, although at times, some folks weren't satisfied;
We'll never forget him, whatever befall,
For God blessed our hearts when he answered our call.

CHASKA, MINNESOTA

I arrived at Chaska during Lent. The year was 1967. The congregation was all in church for the Wednesday night Lenten service. When the service was over a few of the members came over to the parsonage to welcome us. They had arranged to have our family stay at two different homes, the boys at one and the girls at the other. The next morning the moving truck appeared, and several of the members came over to help us unpack. Here again, the office was one room in the parsonage. The next week, the mayor and Rotary President Dr. Ed Ziegler stopped by the parsonage and invited me to come to the next Rotary meeting. I went, and joined the club. Also, Dr. Ziegler became both my friend and my dentist.

At this time, Jonathan was just getting started. When I met Henry McKnight, the founder of Jonathan, he took me for a ride in his Cadillac through the hills of Jonathan. There were no roads or homes there yet. As we drove, he pointed out the features he would like to see. One community was to be built around a college, another around a commercial area, and another around a school.

Another was built around a golf course, and Hazeltine was already there. "And there," he said, "is the highest point in the area—there will be a church there."

Now nobody knew exactly what Jonathan would look like. But the merchants in downtown Chaska were fearful that this Jonathan would ruin their business. Well, I was the Program Chairman for Rotary, so I invited Henry to come and speak to the Rotarians. He came and, along with a slide show, he explained what Jonathan would look like, and this broke the ice between the downtown merchants and Jonathan.

While I was at Chaska, I got the ministers' association to begin holding a Thanksgiving-eve ecumenical service. The first few years we rotated churches, but we finally settled on holding the services at the Catholic church, as the other churches were just too small. I remember being in the balcony of the Catholic church directing an ecumenical choir as we rehearsed for the Thanksgiving-eve service.

Having just finished the new building in West Salem, I received my call to Chaska with a note attached: "Just do the same thing in Chaska." There was certainly a great need for an addition to the church, but former pastors just could not get them to act on it. So as they began to talk about a new addition, I took some deliberate steps to move the conversation along. At this time there was one man who was the new-church guy for most of the Protestant churches that were being built in America. He had written a book, *When You Build Your Church,* which was very popular. So I ordered enough copies of that book to give one to each member of the joint board, of the Christian Education committee and the women's groups. Then at each meeting I would have them discuss one chapter. Now John Scotford was by this time retired, and living in New York. But I contacted him and asked if I could get him and his wife to make a visit to Chaska. He agreed. So when he came, I had him meet with as many of the church groups as possible on Friday and Saturday. Then he preached on Sunday morning and he spoke at a special meeting Sunday afternoon. Now it was just a coincidence that the need here at Chaska was almost identical to the need at West Salem: a building sitting on the left side of the sanctuary, connected at the front; rooms for a church office, a pastor's study, Sunday School rooms, a kitchen and fellowship hall plus restrooms; and, most important of all, a vestibule where people could meet and greet one another. At Chaska, you had to enter the sanctuary through the bell tower, which was not nearly large enough for any conversation or fellowship. Of course I had the plans from West Salem memorized, so it wasn't hard to draw a floor plan for the Chaska addition. I drew it up, a little larger and more expensive than West Salem. Then I mailed that plan to the members, put it in the newsletter, and had it published in the *Chaska Herald*. I had the women help plan the kitchen. Eventually we held a church council and there was a vote to build. This meant we would sell the old parsonage, to be removed from the lot, as that was where the new addition would be built. Then we had to acquire land and build a new parsonage. The vote passed, and we were on our way.

The parsonage had to be moved, and fortunately we found someone who would buy it and move it to a lot he owned on Stoughton Avenue, where he relocated it. At the same time, one of the members took the board up to some lots he owned, and asked us which lot we wanted as his donation to the project. We picked out a lot which had been part of his father's farm, and hired a contractor to build a new parsonage. We now hired an architect who, using my plans, made blueprints for the building. He also helped us find a contractor whom he knew, so we awarded him the contract. Then we needed a financial campaign to raise the money. Since I had done that at West Salem with some help, I could put a fundraising campaign together.

As work on the building progressed, I was over there every day to check on things. One day a block layer was working on the wall between the office and the study. He had finished the wall up to about four feet. When I told him there was a doorway in that wall he said, "No, there isn't," so I said to him, "Go look at your plans." When he came back, he had to take down half of the wall to correct it.

We laid the cornerstone in 1969. I put a lot of different things in the cornerstone: a list of members, a copy of *The Moravian,* several copies of the *Chaska Herald,* and a *Moravian Daily Texts* book. I invited Bishop Mewaldt to come and help me lay the cornerstone. We just dapped a little cement on it—there was a real mason who took it from us and really laid it in the wall. A little later, when the building was finished, I moved my office there. That was the very first time that I had a study that was not in the parsonage.

OTHER PROFESSIONAL OPPORTUNITIES

I retired from Chaska and the pastoral ministry in 1971, and Wylie Pianos and Organs was my first job after that. I stayed there until my salary ran out and I was to go on commission. I knew that wouldn't work, as the other guy had been there many years, and he could play the piano. So I went to a job placement agency, Mark Personnel, and they hired me. We called companies to see if they had any jobs, and then we would try to place people who came to our office in one of those jobs.

Well, I placed one guy in a job at Triple A, the auto club. I soon found out that he was earning more than I was. So I left Mark Personnel and went to the auto club. There we worked from about 5 p.m. until 9 calling people, going right through the Minneapolis phone book, trying to sell them a Triple A membership. We would put a 12-minute recording on the phone stressing the benefits of membership. If they bought with a credit card, we would sign them right on the phone. If they didn't have a credit card, we would set a time when we could stop by their house to deliver the membership and collect their check. One month I sold 100 memberships. That was rare, so I joined the Century Club, and the President took me out for dinner one night.

After two years there, I found that I could sell on the phone pretty well, and I heard that the Foley Company was hiring phone people. So I went over there and got a job. This was not cold calling — the company advertised in a lot of men's magazines and sent a series of three mailers to people who responded to the ads. If, after all three mailers, people still hadn't bought, Foley would give their names to us to call. We were selling machines to sharpen saws. The idea was that our customers would buy a package of machines from us, and then set themselves up to have a business of sharpening saws. We would invite them to Minneapolis for a week of training at our school. A package of machines would cost from $3,000 to seven or eight thousand dollars. I would usually sell two or three packages a day. One time they put a "spiff," a bonus, on each carbide package we sold. So I stopped selling anything else and concentrated on carbide sets. The "spiff" was $50, and I sold 17 carbide packages during the time it was on. I also earned as bonuses a snow blower, a lawn mower, two bicycles, a picnic basket, and several other things. But after about five years there, I wanted something different, so I got hired to sell the Dale Carnegie Course. That didn't go very well, so I quit after three months. Then I got several phone sales jobs, selling tires, copper, advertising. Those baby spoons where you put the medicine in the handle had just come out, so I sold them to drug stores. I was taking phone calls from people who wanted to place a want-ad in the *Star Tribune*. It worked quite well.

But then I made contact with the guy whom I had put into AAA, and he had just started a real estate company in South St. Paul. And he offered me a job. Well, I joined him, and I stayed in real estate for 28 years. Exceptions were four years at the Cokesbury Bookstore and seven years at the CAP food shelf in Shakopee.

CHAPTER
20

COKESBURY
BOOKSTORE

The Cokesbury Bookstore was a book and church supply store owned by the United Methodist Church. It was located in St. Anthony, just north of Minneapolis. It had all the official Methodist supplies, curriculum and other exclusive Methodist merchandise. Other churches could buy from us, but all the Methodist Churches in Minnesota and Wisconsin had to get this merchandise from us.

This store was new in Minnesota, so I went down to Nashville to interview for the job. When I got back, I had to hire four employees to work for me. When we sold choir robes, I would go out to the church at choir rehearsal time. Then I would measure each member and record the size, so each one had a robe that was made just for that person. Beside choir robes and books, we sold communion sets, baptismal fonts, offering plates, clergy robes and stoles. When we sold pew cushions to a church with curved pews, I would go out to the church and make a pattern for each pew, as none of them were exactly alike. I would do that by putting a roll of paper the length of the pew and pressing it in between the seat and the back, and of course numbering each pew and each pattern.

The church had its annual meeting once a year at the college in Mankato. I would always set up quite a large bookstore, a hundred boxes of books or more, as it was a good chance for the ministers to pick up a couple of books that they had been wanting. I hired a college student to help me sell books for a few hours each day. I always had a chance to address the assembly and pitch a few of my books. And then I would present to the bishop a check for many thousands of dollars, because all the profits from the book store went to the United Methodist Church in Minnesota. Since all the pastors got to know me, I had many requests to fill in for them at their church for vacations or other times they would be away. During those four years, I preached at over 40 United Methodist Churches in the Twin Cities area.

CAP AGENCY
FOOD SHELF

At the food shelf in Shakopee, I was the first full-time paid manager. Along with volunteers, we gave food to about 25 families each day. People could come once a month, but about eight times each month I gave people a second order if it was an emergency. We had a truck to go out to schools, stores, banks, and other places who had collected food for us. Then I had some money that I used at Cooper's supermarket for things we were short of. At Thanksgiving time we gave an entire meal, including a turkey, to those who needed help. I often packed the boxes in the John Hus room at the Moravian Church. I would ask my real estate friends from the nearby Burnet office to come over the day before to pack the boxes. At Christmas time I had barrels at all the banks and some other places where people could drop off unwrapped toys. Then I collected all these and took them to the Moravian Church. We had thousands of toys, so on a certain day parents could come and shop for toys for their children at no charge.

Besides the food shelf, I managed three other food

distribution programs. In NAPS, Nutrition Assistance Program for Seniors, we took food to 12 senior independent-living facilities where each person did their own cooking. MAC was a program for Mother and Child; they came to the food shelf to get this food.

Then there was the USDA Commodities program. For years the government had been buying up food to support the farmers, so they had several huge warehouses full of food. This Commodity program gave out butter, cheese, flour and canned goods. Every month I had a semi bring a load of this food to the K-Mart warehouse near the food shelf in Shakopee. They brought the food in on a Friday. Then on Saturday my 12 sets of volunteers would come to the warehouse to get a load of food. They came from Shakopee, Chaska, Chanhassen, Waconia, Watertown, and other towns in Carver and Scott Counties. Each team took the food to their location, and those who were signed up for the program came to get their food. These four programs gave away a lot of food to needy families, so I had 70 volunteers whom I had recruited, trained and managed. I worked there for seven years, and I loved every minute of it. But after that I resigned and went back to real estate.

REAL ESTATE

I got into real estate almost by accident. I went over to visit Mike, the guy whom I had sent to Triple A for a job. I found out that he had just started his own real estate company in South St. Paul. He had four agents and was looking for two more. I would have to take all the training and pass the state test to become licensed. I said I would be happy to join him.

The classes and test took about a month. Then I was licensed and ready to go to work. I met a contractor who let me take his whole subdivision exclusively. I sold maybe twenty homes and two lots for him. Then I had him build a house for me, right in the middle of the development. In all, I sold more than 30 homes for him.

Then one day I was talking to an agent from the Burnet real estate company. He told me that I would have far more opportunities with a larger company, so he talked me into joining Burnet. I started with them at their St. Paul office. But then the manager of the Roseville office heard about me, and he convinced me to go to work for him at Roseville. I was doing real well at Roseville when one of the owners of the company asked me to be the manager of our Woodbury office. I accepted his offer. But

Woodbury then was just a small office, and I had made more money selling than I was paid to be a manager. And managers were not allowed to sell. So after a short time I resigned the manager position, but I stayed at that office for some time. Then they opened a new office in West St. Paul. That was much closer to my home, so I transferred there. One night the company hired Johnny Cash to give a private show just for our company. He had been in the Twin Cities that week, so we could get him on Saturday night for less money. Well, after the show, I was talking to an older lady whom I liked very much. She was the manager at Minnetonka and she talked me into transferring to her office. She almost made me her assistant there. I had a private office, while about 15 other agents worked in the bullpen a single large room. And she had me teach some training classes for the other agents. But then she left to go to Rochester to open some new Burnet offices there. And by that time, Burnet had an office in Chaska, so I moved to that office. While I was there, I did quite a few weddings in our conference room. I would walk past the agents' offices to get a couple of agents to be witnesses before I could pronounce them husband and wife. I worked out of the Chaska office for eleven years and then, in 2005, I retired from real estate.

I did quite well in real estate. I enjoyed the work, meeting with people. And I was quite successful. I was always in the top ten agents in the company, and I was rewarded for it. Among other awards I won were a gold ring, a gold watch, a silver tray, some silver beer mugs with glass bottoms, a set of pewter wine goblets, a huge loving cup, a desk set, several thermometers, pens, clocks, paper weights, and many wall plaques. So I have many souvenirs to remind me of many happy days in real estate.

THE SALVATION ARMY

I was always interested in the Salvation Army, its history and mission. During the time that I was selling real estate at the Chaska office I learned a lot more about the Army. I went to a couple of their meetings here in Chaska, and soon I was the volunteer Salvation Army Carver County Chairman. With this went a number of responsibilities. First was to manage the Red Kettle Campaign. This went from Thanksgiving until Christmas. I only had two kettles in Chaska, one at Cooper's and one at Target. The one at Cooper's kind of took care of itself. Gary Cooper was dedicated enough to the cause that he had his employees handle the kettle, standing outside ringing a bell and thanking people when they put money in. I only had to go every other day and collect the money. The kettles were locked with a padlock, and I had the only key.

But Target was a different story. First I had to contact the management to get permission. Then I had to recruit volunteers. We could have the kettle out every day from Thanksgiving to Christmas. Every day was divided up into 2-hour shifts, from 10 in the morning until 8 at night. That was a lot of shifts to fill. I got musical groups from the schools and some people from church; a few heard about it and called me to volunteer. I just couldn't get enough volunteers to fill every slot, even though some took more than one. I had to be there at the start of each shift to get the kettle out (they let us store the kettle and tripod in the store) and show them what to do. Everyone wore a red apron and had a little bell to ring. Then about twice a day, I would come down to empty the kettle. Once in a while, they would call me to come down because the kettle was full. I would unlock it, put the money in a Target bag and take it home. Then I quickly counted it, estimating the amount of change. When I had a few bags, I would take them down to the First National Bank in Chaska. My treasurer worked there—I don't know what she did, but she had her own private office. If she wasn't there, I just put the bags in her office. When she had quite a few, she would deposit the money into our Carver County Salvation Army account on which she could write checks.

My other responsibility was getting that money to the people who needed it. In those days there were a lot of needy people wandering the streets, and they often stopped at one of the churches to get help. But the churches didn't have money to help them, so I contacted all the church receptionists and secretaries and told them to call me when somebody came in and I would immediately come down to meet the people at the church, interview them and see what I could offer them. Sometimes it was a referral to the food shelf, or maybe to the thrift shop for clothes. The thrift shop normally sold for a minimal price, but I could arrange for these people to go over there and shop for free. Maybe it was a referral to the County social services. But I could also help them with food from Cooper's, gas from SuperAmerica, or prescriptions from Target. I did this by using vouchers. I would give the merchant a voucher for the required amount, and the merchant would mail this to my treasurer and she would send them a check. But my biggest use of vouchers was for giving these people a place to stay for the night. Otherwise they would sleep on park benches or in their cars. I had arrangements at the two local motels, the one on Yellow Brick Road and the other on Highway 169. I would just call them, give them the name, how many in the family, how many days I would cover, and when they would come in. Then I would go to the motel the next day and give them a voucher. They always gave me a discount because I had so much volume. They just had to mail the voucher to my treasurer at the bank, and she would send them a check. Hardly a week went by that I didn't have at least one family in a motel.

One time I had a family with a special need. They were living in a bus converted into living quarters. But they had a flat tire and they were parked in the parking lot of the Chaska Kindergarten Center. Now there was no overnight parking allowed there, but they couldn't move. So I called the Chaska Chief of Police to ask him if he would tell his patrolmen to not bother them that night. That was okay with him. But as soon as we hung up, he went out there himself to see the situation! An hour later, he sent his son out there with a brand-new tire and he installed it on the bus. What a guy!

I had one other tough problem, but we solved it. This lady who lived down on Stoughton Avenue had just brought her newborn baby home from the hospital, but the baby had to be monitored 24 hours a day over the phone. Trouble was she hadn't paid her phone bill for some time, and they were going to disconnect her phone at 6 p.m. that night. And the phone office was in St. Louis. I went over to my treasurer's office, and she called the phone company to see if they would give the woman a few more days. They refused.

What if we mailed them a check yet that night? No, they wouldn't accept that. She and I pondered how to solve the problem. Finally I suggested that we put it on my credit card. She called them back, gave them my credit card numbers, and they accepted that. Problem solved. Not quite. When I got home, I found out that the credit card company had blocked my account. I didn't usually pay for a telephone bill in St. Louis, so they assumed that the card had been stolen. It took a little explaining, but they finally reinstated my card.

Well, after ten years of doing this I decided to resign, so they planned a farewell party for me. Some of the Salvation Army officers came out, and there was a meal. Then they presented me with a nice green plant and an Appreciation Certificate. That certificate is still hanging on the wall in my office. And during this time, I sold homes to two of my Salvation Army friends.

MY WEDDING MINISTRY

Through the years of my retirement, I have conducted what I call my wedding ministry. I don't advertise it that way, but that is the way I consider it. When I left the pastoral ministry, I had done 46 weddings. Most of our churches have older people, so funerals are more common than weddings. But after I retired, I thought that doing weddings would be a good thing to do. I was now registered, licensed in four states: North Dakota, Wisconsin, Illinois and Minnesota. So I advertised a little, and I went to get acquainted with the girls in both Chaska and Shakopee who give out marriage licenses, so they would refer people to me. I found that most members of a church would go to their own pastor to be married. But there were lots of people who had no church and didn't know any pastors. Some couldn't even speak English. But I figured I would ask no questions; if they could get a license at the courthouse and had two witnesses, I would marry them. If necessary, I would even supply the witnesses. Tom and Marvel Heath have been witnesses for about 12 weddings for me.

Well, it worked out quite well. Many years I did 50 or 60 weddings. In all, as of this writing, I have done

457 weddings. So there was a real need for this service. In order to be sure I got as many referrals as possible, twice a year I would put together boxes of wrapped candy and give a box to each courthouse staff, at Chaska and at Shakopee. That way they got to know me personally, and were glad to refer people to me.

A couple weddings were rather unique. After one wedding held outside in Arlington, it was obvious that the people were Christian, Lutheran, yet they asked me to do the wedding. While walking to my car after the wedding, the bride's mother walked with me. She said, "I suppose you wonder why we didn't have our own pastor from town do the wedding. Well, we knew he would refuse, because the two kids had been living together for a few months. And in the Missouri Synod Lutheran Church, he just would not marry them."

Another unique wedding was in Waconia. The morning after the wedding, the groom's mother called me and asked, "Can you cancel this wedding? Last night the bride left here and went home to her father in St. Paul." Well, I had completed the license and put it in my mailbox ready to be picked up, but it was still there. So I told the mother to meet me at the courthouse in half an hour, I went and pulled the license out of my mailbox, and met them at the courthouse. I told the clerk there what had happened, and she took it and said she would cancel it. That was close.

I call this my wedding ministry. Here's why. I have married all kinds of people: Catholics, Protestants, Christians, non-Christians, Jews, Muslims, Hindus, and those with no religion. I never ask what they are;

sometimes it comes out, and sometimes it doesn't. But to every couple I marry, I give a wrapped gift of a framed copy of Warner Sallman's picture, "The Head of Christ," probably the most well-known picture ever painted. I buy them from the publisher, 24 at a time. Then I get the frames from Target, frame them, and wrap them 12 at a time. Every couple gets one. I don't know what they do with them, but a few couples have thanked me for them, saying, "We put in on the wall by our front door" or "We have it on a nightstand in our bedroom." Perhaps some people throw them away, but at least they have been touched a little bit by looking at this picture of Christ. And one couple I married joined the Chaska Moravian Church. This has been my wedding ministry.

CHAPTER
25

MORAVIAN MUSIC

My whole life long, I have been interested in music, particularly Moravian music. I have directed bands and choirs at almost every church I served, and I have cut and pasted many Moravian songs in order to get the music that I needed for a particular event.

It began when I was in the primary class in Sunday School at the Moravian Church in Sturgeon Bay, Wisconsin. Our longtime, renowned organist and choir director, Hugh MacLean, was preparing us kids for the Christmas program, and helping us boys to learn to sing the alto to "Jesus Loves Me." "That's very good, boys," Hugh would say, "but that first note in the third measure is only a half step down, just a teeny bit lower that what you were singing. And also, that's a quarter note—looks like a cherry with a stem on it" (after all, we were in Door County, Cherryland!) "so you don't hold it very long."

When I got a little older, I could go to our youth meetings every Sunday night. In summer, we would drive out to someone's cottage on Lake Michigan for our meetings. At first, we sang Moravian Chorales from a little brown booklet, *Selected Moravian Chorales,* published in 1933 by the Moravian Young People's Conference of the Western District. Here we sang 68 A, 82 D, and 115 B, better known as "Jesus, Still Lead On," "Jesus Makes My Heart Rejoice," and "How Great the Bliss to be a Sheep of Jesus." Then, in 1942, the church published the *Moravian Youth Hymnal.* My brother Norman made a special wooden box with a handle on it for carrying the Youth Hymnals out to our meetings, and we also had a suitcase-type portable pump organ that we lugged out in the woods. On a Sunday night, anyone nearby could hear our organ playing and us singing "'Tis the Most Blest and Needful Part" as the music wafted across the shores and over the waters of Lake Michigan.

Finally I was old enough to go to Camp Chetek. Here, Rudy Schultze usually was the music leader, and I always sang in the camp choir. On Sunday afternoons, we would put on a choir concert. But in certain years, we were especially lucky when Ed Mickey from the Southern Province would come and be our music leader. "Careful there, boys," Ed would say. "Let's have fun, but let's get it right!"

I spent 50 weeks of my life at church camps. Twenty-five at Chetek, first as camper, then as counselor, then as teacher, then as campfire leader, and finally as assistant director. Then I was director for numerous other camps, Winmor and Inmormindo. For the Wisconsin Council of Churches, I directed several years of family camps, and they also asked me to lead a camp for church camping leaders, to teach them about church camping. I was also at Tar Hollow and Inabah in the Eastern District. So church camping has been a huge part of my life.

During my years in Bethlehem for college and

seminary, I usually attended the West Side Church, and was part of that awesome West Side Youth Group. We always met two or three times a week, Sunday nights for our regular youth meeting, then once or so for a wiener roast or other such fun. John Groenfeldt was our pastor— he was a Sturgeon Bay boy. Ted Hartman was the choir director, and his father was the organist. How often during our choir rehearsals on Thursday nights, Ted would say, "You basses aren't getting it quite right there in the third line. Dad, play just the bass part for them."

Thor Johnson is without doubt the most notable name in Moravian music in modern times. Thor was an idol of mine. He instituted the annual Moravian Music Festivals, and I sang under him at the festival of 1957 held in Bethlehem. I remember one hot Sunday afternoon when we were rehearsing in the balcony of Central Church. By chance I was standing next to the orchestra, and the violin player sitting next to me needed someone to turn pages for him. So I got to turn pages for him. His name was Isaac Stern.

When I got out into the pastorate, I assembled and directed an Easter band at each church I served. But I found that there was a need for usable music for band, since the books were scarce and out of print. So I took all the hymns needed for Easter Sunrise, Easter morning, Christmas, and several more, and cut and pasted (not today's computer cut-and-paste, but with a copy machine, a scissors and glue) until I had made band music for all the hymns in the seven different parts needed for band. The band would often play before church services each Sunday in Lent, each Sunday in Advent, and other times throughout the year.

As pastor at West Salem, Illinois, I would get up on Easter morning about 3 a.m. and play recorded Easter chorales from the speaker in the bell tower, letting the whole town know that the Moravians were getting ready to celebrate the resurrection of Christ. Also while at West Salem, I met a Lutheran pastor who invited me to bring our choir to his church to introduce his people to Moravian music. So I put together a program including "Hearken," "It is a Blessed Thing," "Morning Star," "Hosanna," "Jesus, Still Lead On," "O Sacred Head, Now Wounded," and others. It was so successful that other pastors began to invite us to come to their churches and perform. "Give us supper," I said, "and the offering is yours." What wonderful times for the choir members and their families as we "went on the road."

So you see, Moravian music has long been an important area of my life, and I treasure the numerous Moravian music CDs that have been given to me.

CHAPTER
26

MY LIFE

Well, there you have it. The story of my life. It's been anything but boring. I was given a lot of opportunities, and I took advantage of most of them. I have found joy in everything I did, especially in helping other people who had great needs. I have been privileged to have been able to find the resources to make that possible. I am grateful for each day of my life, as I am grateful to each of you for your understanding and love.

—Dad

CHAPTER 27

HOW OLD ARE YOU?

Age is a quality of mind,
If you have left your dreams behind,
If hope is cold,
If you no longer look ahead,
If your ambitions' fires are dead—
Then you are old.

But if from life you take the best,
And if in life you keep the jest,
If love you hold;
No matter how the years go by,
No matter how the birthdays fly—
You are not old.

—H.S. Fritsch

PART II

MEDITATIONS

The following are several meditations I have written that I want to share with you. Some of them have been previously published in newspapers and booklets. Most of them I wrote for a book that I hope to publish in the near future. The name of the book will be *Sermons From the Door,* consisting of meditations based on people, places and events from Door County, Wisconsin. I hope these meditations will be meaningful to you.

CASTLES IN THE SAND

It was one of those magnificent August days, warm and still, with just a trace of clouds in the sky, the kind of day children live for. We were spending the entire day on the beach, swimming in the bay, running on the stones and building castles in the sand—beautiful castles, gorgeous structures with towers and walls and moats. We could almost see King Arthur and his knights marching on the upper deck. Oh, what a beautiful day, beautiful castles, beautiful sand.

Later that afternoon the air began to chill as a breeze began to stir in the trees. Before long the bay was wild with foam, and our ears were filled with the roar of whitecaps breaking on the shore. Our beautiful sand castles were quickly flattened by the waves.

That evening after dark, dressed in sweaters to protect us against the cold and the wind, we stood again on the shore. Looking out over the water, we saw familiar lights our father had taught us to know—Peshtigo Reef, the Green Bay channel markers, and just beyond Potawatomi Park, the Sherwood Point Lighthouse.

The wind was still blowing. The waves were still rolling. But the lighthouse stood undaunted. The same shore, the same wind, the same waves. But while our castles in the sand were flattened, the lighthouse stood straight and secure, sending out its comforting beam.

"Why?" my childish mind wondered. What was the difference? Then it came to me. The castles were built on sand, but the lighthouse was built on rock.

Jesus taught us that we could build our lives on either the sand or the rock. To those who chose sand, He said the storms of life would erode and tear down. But to those who chose to build their lives upon the rock, He promised that they would withstand and endure forever.

Christ Himself is our Rock! Even Christians will have times when the waves roll furiously over their lives, and anxiously we watch whitecaps tumbling in upon our shores. But we will be ever upheld and sustained because of His promise, *"It fell not: for it was founded upon a rock."* (Matthew 7:25)

MINISTARE

I am extremely fortunate to have been born in Sturgeon Bay, Door County, Wisconsin. I also feel fortunate to have been able to do all of my schooling, kindergarten through high school, in the same building. The old school was located on the corner of 5th and Michigan. After the building was no longer suitable for use as a school, it became a YWCA for some time, and a few years ago it was demolished.

To me, it was a perfect school facility. It had everything: labs, shops, rooms for each elementary grade, study halls, high school classrooms, offices, plus a huge gym with a stage on one end, and a huge auditorium seating perhaps five or six hundred or more. Up front was a fully equipped stage, with curtains, wings, and everything needed to produce a good play. Through my 13 years at that building, I was no stranger to the wings and the stage. While in kindergarten, I was selected to appear in one of the high school plays, in which I played a young Dutch boy who put out his wooden shoes waiting for St. Nicholas to fill them with Christmas gifts. I also had to learn to skip so that I could skip around with my older sister.

Through my elementary years, we put on many

programs and plays from that stage, and in high school I performed in many choir and band concerts. I played the drums, especially the timpani. Beginning in eighth grade, I was in Tom Runkel's pit orchestra, so I saw each play many times over. Our high school senior class play was "Tons of Money," in which I played an attorney, Chesterton, of Chesterton, Chesterton, and Chesterton.

But the most significant thing about that stage, the thing that has gone with me my whole life, was the emblem on the stage curtains. That same emblem also appeared on our high school class rings. Around the edge were the words, "Sturgeon Bay High School," and inside was a balancing scale for justice, a lamp for knowledge, and on a banner across the emblem was inscribed the Latin word, "Ministare." *Ministare,* to minister, to serve. Surely a high school can put no finer challenge before its graduates than this, to go out into the world and minister, and serve. Serve the needy, serve the oppressed, serve the downtrodden. Minister to the ignorant, to the hungry, to the thirsty, to the ill, to those in prison, to those without parents, to those without anybody—the lost and lonely in the world. Go minister, go serve.

And so we, of the high school class of 1945, did go out and serve. I became a minister of the Gospel. Others ministered through teaching, through the practice of medicine, or law, or social services, or business or finance. Some ministered through farming, or simply by being a parent to their own children or the children of others.

The King James version of the Bible says in Mark 10:45, *"For even the Son of man came not to be ministered* unto, *but to minister, and to give his life a ransom for many."* In newer versions we read, *"For even the Son of Man came not to be served but to serve, and to give his life as a ransom for many."* Our Lord gave his life in service to the blind, the lame, the ill, the hungry, the fearful, the lost, the children. There is no finer path in life than to follow in his way. The world is filled with opportunities. Go, minister. Go serve. *"Ministare."*

UNCLE HENRY

Uncle Henry Maples was not really my uncle. Actually, we were not related at all. But he might as well have been my uncle, as he was an old friend of my family, both of my grandparents and my parents. We would often go to his home to visit with him and his wife Anna. Uncle Henry worked in a hardware store, a store with shelves and drawers of merchandise all along with walls going high up to the ceiling. In front of the shelves was a ladder with wheels on a track. You could roll the ladder close to the items you needed, and then climb up to get them. Uncle Henry had wonderful stories to tell; he had been around the world with lots of fascinating experiences. But one of his most interesting stories happened right here in Door County.

The Friends Church of Sturgeon Bay, a Quaker church, is located on Maple Street in what was formerly known as Sawyer, now the West Side. In the winter of 1913, the church was sponsoring a series of revival services, and the guest preacher was the Rev. George Bennard. Bennard had been a Salvation Army officer, but now he was a Methodist minister and evangelist. Not only was he a lively preacher but he was also a musician, and he knew the power of a swinging melody, a good chorus, and easily learned words.

During those days, Bennard was working on writing a new song. In the evening after his meetings, he would go to his room and put together words with his tune. At that time, the parsonage for the Friends Church was located on the first floor of the building, with the church upstairs. That is where the two pastors, Frank and Estella McCann, lived. Late in the afternoon of January 12, 1913, as a number of guests had gathered together in the parsonage, Rev. Bennard got up from his rocking chair and said, "I've got something that I have been working on. Let's try it out and see how it is." As he brought some new music, he asked the sister of one of the pastors to play the organ and sing alto. He himself carried the melody. A visiting pastor who was helping with the revival sang tenor, and Uncle Henry was asked to sing the bass. And the world heard for the first time the beloved words of a new song:

On a hill far away, stood an old rugged cross,
The emblem of suffering and shame,
And I love that old cross, where the dearest and best
For a world of lost sinners was slain.
So I'll cherish the old, rugged cross,
'Til my trophies at last I lay down;
I will cling to the old, rugged cross,
And exchange it someday for a crown.

In 1947, a memorial was dedicated to commemorate the writing of this song. Erected beside the church, the memorial consists of a huge cross made of Western fir timbers, and at its base, a Bible carved from mahogany wood. A brass plaque is engraved with the details of the writing of what many feel is the world's most popular Christian hymn, "The Old Rugged Cross." Residents as well as visitors to Sturgeon Bay are invited to drive by the church on Maple Street on the West Side. You may park your car on the street, get out, walk over to the memorial and pay your respects to the cross and the Saviour who gave his life on it.

The Apostle Paul, writing to the Corinthians in I Corinthians 1:18, wrote: *"For the preaching of the cross is to them that perish foolishness; but unto us which are saved it is the power of God."* Bennard's message in song, written in 1913, still rings true today, the cross of Jesus Christ.

While the body of Abraham Lincoln lay in state in Cleveland, an elderly black woman stood in line holding a young child in her arms. After a long look at the face of the emancipator, the woman whispered to the child, "Take a long look, honey. Dat man died for you."

These words are also the words that give meaning to the cross. "Dat man died for you." At the cross we see God's broken heart. At the cross we see Christ's victory. At the cross we see God's forgiving love and our victory over death.

"For the preaching of the cross is to them that perish foolishness; but unto us which are saved it is the power of God."

So I'll cherish the old, rugged cross,
'Til my trophies at last I lay down;
I will cling to the old, rugged cross,
And exchange it someday for a crown.

FATHER BOB

"I'll be doing about the same thing, but in a different church."

It was one of the last days of our senior year in high school, and my friend, Bob Baudhuin, and I were talking with our chemistry teacher. Mr. Steinhoff said to us, "Al, I know you are going to study for the ministry, but Bob, what will you be doing?" "I'll be doing about the same thing, but in a different church.'

I had gone to the public elementary school in Sturgeon Bay, while Bob had attended St. Joseph's Catholic School. Bob was a Catholic, and I was a Moravian, but we got along very well, and the following summer we worked together.

Bob was my helper on the milk truck. Working for Pleck's, the local dairy, each morning we loaded up a huge stake truck with wooden barrels. Each barrel held 27 quarts of milk in glass quart bottles. We filled the barrels with ice and covered them with a canvas lid. Then we would drive our truck up and down the peninsula, stopping at each store, restaurant, and motel. During the summer, so many visitors would be in the County that the businesses did not begin to have enough refrigerated space to hold all the milk they needed for each day. So we would stop at each business, unload tubs of milk and roll them under the shade of a tree in the back yard, to be their supply of milk for the day.

Of course, some stops were more fun than others. We had a great time delivering to the girls' camp that used to be located near the Fish Creek entrance to Peninsula State Park. There were a number of college-aged girls on the staff, some of whom we got to know quite well. But our favorite stop was at the Brookside Tea Gardens in Ephraim. Mrs. Paschke's two daughters were often there, and they would even get up into the truck to help us unload. Then, we were often invited into the kitchen and offered plates heaped with delicious Door County home cooking.

When summer ended, we each went our own ways: I to Moravian College and Seminary in Bethlehem, Pennsylvania, and Bob to Maryknoll College in New York. After graduation, I was sent to preach at Moravian churches in North Dakota, while Bob went off to do missionary work, first in Taiwan and later in the islands of Indonesia. I eagerly looked forward to his Christmas card each year. And about every three or four years, we would end up visiting Door County at the same time, when we would meet and enjoy coffee or lunch together.

Through the years of a lifetime, Bob, Father Bob, and I shared the same ideals, the same motivations, the same spirit, we worshipped the same God. But we were not able to worship together, at the same place, at the same church. The boundaries of denominationalism kept us from sharing our worship of God. What a sin!

I have always been of an ecumenical mind. When I left North Dakota, I received a letter of appreciation from the leader of the State Council of Churches thanking me for the inter-church efforts I had put forth. While serving in Wisconsin, I volunteered for the State Council of Churches by directing their family camp program, by leading their training camps for church camping leaders, and by leading teams which traveled across the state putting on workshops for Daily Vacation Bible School teachers. Yet, the walls of separation between Christians of various denominations still exist. What will it take before the prayers of our Lord Jesus come to pass, *"Those who believe in me . . . that they may all be one."* (John 17:20-21)

THE GOOD SHEPHERD

After graduation and ordination, both in June of 1951, I was called to serve two churches in North Dakota, Goshen and Casselton. I directly followed my cousin, Howard Nelson, who now had been called to serve the East Moravian Church in Green Bay. So I was familiar with these churches, since I had visited him there several times. In getting organized in the parsonage at Goshen, I found my study to be one of the bedrooms upstairs. I found a used desk, the same one that I still use, in the want ads being sold by a retired pastor in Moorhead, Minnesota. It didn't take long before some of the men of the church took a truck to Moorhead to get the desk. Then I took a trip to Fargo to a religious book store, and there I bought a large, framed picture to hang behind my desk. It was the picture, "The Good Shepherd" by Bernhard Plockhorst, a German painter who was born in 1825 and died in 1907.

You all have seen this picture as it has hung behind my desk in all of the studies I have had, and it still is hanging here in Chaska. I have distributed hundreds of copies of the picture to friends. The picture is based on the story of the good shepherd in John 10:1-16. Jesus, the Good Shepherd, is leading his flock of sheep along a narrow, rugged path. Along the way, one little lamb has gotten a thorn in his leg, and it hurt as he walked. So the good shepherd stopped and picked up the little lamb and is carrying him in his arms.

When I look at the picture, the little lamb is ME. I am just a lamb compared to others who are stronger, wiser, more competent than me, and besides I have a special need, the thorn in my flesh. So Jesus has stopped and picked me up, and I am being carried in his arms. The little lamb is me and every time I look at the picture I am reminded how Jesus has picked me up, with the thorn in my leg, and he is carrying me safe to my home. Jesus to me is a friend, a shepherd, Lord of my life, and my saviour. This picture probably sums up my lifelong faith as well as anything.

"The Lord is my shepherd; I shall not want." (Psalm 23:1)

MEDITATION
6

PORT DES MORTS

"Why," asked friend, "is it called 'Door County' when it seems to be a door to no place?" Indeed, you could almost go a few miles north of Green Bay and put up a sign saying, "No Exit—Dead End!" The answer lies in a little knowledge of geography and some history.

Just off the tip of Door County proper are located five islands. The largest by far is Washington Island. Four smaller ones are Plum Island, Detroit Island, Hog Island and Rock Island. The coastline on both mainland and the islands is shallow, giving no good landing spot for a boat. Furthermore, the coastline is almost completely filled with rocks. In addition, strong currents and fierce winds, blowing in all directions at once, make it extremely difficult to steer a boat safely through the course. And we are thinking of the days before the time of an Evinrude 75-horse motor. Rather, in the early days, many boats were man-powered, with oars, or powered by sails in the wind. Thus, hundreds of ships have crashed on the rocks there, and thousands of sailors have met their death among those winds and rocks. During a single week in September 1872, eight large boats were stranded and wrecked there. The Indians had their own name for the waters, meaning the door of death. When early French Explorers arrived, noticing by personal experience how well the Indians' name fit, they named the waters *"Port des Morts,"* the Door of Death.

The doorway to death! Not something we generally take pleasure in thinking about. Yet death is part of the human experience. The founders of the town of Sturgeon Bay made a place for us to celebrate death years and years ago, when they established the Bayside Cemetery, a beautiful place of grass and trees, just up from the waters of Sturgeon Bay. All four of my grandparents are buried there. My parents are buried there, side by side with my brother. I could not ask for a more beautiful or peaceful spot as their final resting place.

And yet, death is not final; it is not the end. It is only a door through which we must pass. And on the other side? Eternal life with the resurrected body in the presence of our Lord Jesus and our family and friends, all in a new relationship. There will be no marriage there — no sorrow, no sin, no suffering, no illness — but Heaven, with all its glory.

Think of the most beautiful, peaceful, serene place you can imagine. It's Heaven. Sort of like Door County.

"Do not let your hearts be troubled; believe in God, believe also in me. In My Father's house are many dwelling places. If it were not so, would I have told you that I go to prepare a place for you? And if I go and prepare a place for you, I will come again and will take you to myself, so that where I am, there you may be also." (John 14:1-3)

SAY YES

I had just finished giving a talk to the kids at the Catholic school in Burnsville on behalf of the CAP Agency food shelf when one little girl, she may have been seven or 8, came up to me and in a soft, sweet voice said, "Do you take gifts for the food shelf?" I said, "Yes, I do," and she told me, "Once in a while when we are short of money, we have gone to the food shelf for food. Now I have an extra dollar. Can I give it to you for the food shelf?" I accepted her gift and thanked her profusely for her generosity. But I didn't turn that dollar in right away. Instead I used it in my next 50 or so presentations, telling her story and showing her gift of one dollar. The Lord turned that single dollar bill into I don't know how many thousands of dollars, gifts motivated by the generosity of that little seven-year-old.

It was a little after 5 o'clock. The food shelf was closed, the volunteers had left, but I had not yet locked the doors. A woman came in, insisting that I give her some food. But we were closed, and she didn't have an appointment. But she insisted. So I got a shopping cart, went up and down the aisles and put together an order for her. As I was helping her carry it out to her car, she said, "This morning, my electricity was turned off because I didn't have money to pay them. I needed money for a damage deposit on a new apartment, but I didn't have any, so they said No. My car needs repairs, but with no money to pay them, they wouldn't fix it. You are the only person today who said Yes to me." And as I told that story hundreds of times later, to schools, businesses, service clubs and churches, I always said, "The reason I could say Yes to that woman was because you have said Yes to me. Because of your fine donations to the food shelf, I was able to help her out. But in reality, it was you who were saying Yes to her, because you have given the gifts needed so I could help her with food. When you give gifts to the food shelf, you are saying Yes to hundreds of families every week. While so many others say No, together, we can say Yes."

"Come, you that are blessed by my Father, inherit the kingdom prepared for you from the foundation of the world; for I was hungry and you gave me food, I was thirsty and you gave me something to drink, I was a stranger and you welcomed me, I was naked and you gave me clothing, I was sick and you took care of me, I was in prison and you visited me. Then the righteous will answer him, 'Lord, when was it that we saw you hungry and gave you food, or thirsty and gave you something to drink? And when was it that we saw you a stranger and welcomed you, or naked and gave you clothing? And when was it that we saw you sick or in prison and visited you?' And the King will answer them, 'Truly I tell you, just as you did it to one of the least of these who are members of my family, you did it to me.'" (Matthew 25:34-40)

MY MANTRA

While I was at the food shelf, one of the girls I worked with told me how she uses "flash prayers"—just a short, quick prayer for someone. If you see an ambulance with an ill or injured person in it, pray a flash prayer for that person. If you run across a car accident, or any accident at all, pray a flash prayer for the victim. If you are going on a job interview, say a prayer for the person who will be interviewing you. If you're in an audience with a speaker, say a prayer for the speaker. Got the idea? It will help you as much as the person you are praying for.

Those who practice yoga, while doing their exercises, commonly repeat a word or phrase over and over again, a word called a mantra. I have found a mantra to use, not while doing yoga, but while meditating. The mantra is "Jesus is Lord." Accent on the first and last syllables. JEsus is LORD. Actually, these words were the first creed of the early Christian church. Before they had any formalized creeds, like the Apostles' Creed, the Nicene Creed or the Athanasian Creed, early Christians believed that these three words expressed the entirety of their faith, that Jesus Christ their Saviour was Lord and Master of their lives. All that was expressed in the words, Jesus is Lord.

When they met one another on the street, they would say "Jesus is Lord," and the response would be, "Jesus is Lord."

Sometimes when I am praying or meditating, I may just be too tired to think of what I want to pray for. So I just repeat over and over, Jesus is Lord. Jesus is Lord. And really, those words are the very heart of my faith. Jesus is Lord.

THE PRAYER OF ST. FRANCIS

No, I did not write this prayer. We really don't know who did. But it has been ascribed to St. Francis of Assisi, and it would match his life style. So let's give him credit for it.

It has become my favorite prayer, which I first discovered while in Seminary. I have prayed it and used it in services and in writings, hundreds if not thousands of times. And as I close this story of my life, I want to share it with you now.

Lord, make me an instrument of Your peace,
Where there is hatred, let me sow love;
Where there is injury, pardon;
Where there is discord, harmony;
Where there is error, truth;
Where there is doubt, faith;
Where there is despair, hope;
Where there is darkness, light;
Where there is sadness, joy.
O Divine Master, Grant that I may not so much seek
To be consoled as to console;

To be understood as to understand;
To be loved as to love.
For it is in giving that we receive;
It is in pardoning that we are pardoned;
And it is in dying that we are born to eternal life.

Made in the USA
Charleston, SC
07 December 2014